P9-CRZ-791

FACTS AND COMMENTS

FACTS AND COMMENTS

BY

HERBERT SPENCER

Essay Index Reprint Series

BOOKS FOR LIBRARIES PRESS
FREEPORT, NEW YORK

Gardner Webb College Library

First Published 1902
Reprinted 1970

INTERNATIONAL STANDARD BOOK NUMBER:
0-8369-1853-3

LIBRARY OF CONGRESS CATALOG CARD NUMBER:
70-128314

PRINTED IN THE UNITED STATES OF AMERICA

B
1653
F34
1970

950

Direct

11-3-70

PREFACE.

DURING the years spent in writing various systematic works, there have from time to time arisen
ideas not fitted for incorporation in them. Many of
these have found places in articles published in reviews, and are now collected together in the three
volumes of my essays. But there remain a number
which have not yet found expression: some of them
relatively trivial, some of more interest, and some
which I think are important.

I have felt reluctant to let these pass unrecorded,
and hence during the last two years, at intervals now
long and now short, have set them down in the following pages. Possibly to a second edition I shall
make some small additions, but, be this as it may, the
volume herewith issued I can say with certainty will
be my last.

H. S.

BRIGHTON, *March*, 1902.

v

CONTENTS.

viii CONTENTS.

FACTS AND COMMENTS.

A BUSINESS–PRINCIPLE.

AMONG the many cases of malpractices by solicitors recently brought to light, one is especially striking as seeming at variance with all probability. To suppose that a solicitor who has been President of The Incorporated Law Society and also chairman of its Disciplinary Committee could be guilty of diverting to his own use large sums belonging to clients, seems contrary to common sense. "Surely here is a man who may be implicitly trusted," would be the remark made to any one who doubted the wisdom of giving him unchecked administrative power. As we see, however, the scepticism would have been justified.

Not unfrequently I have been astonished at the confidence with which men deliver their securities and the control of important transactions to their legal agents. "Everybody does it," each thinks to himself, "and I suppose I may safely do it." This unlimited trust seems the more remarkable after considering the utter absence of trust shown by the

1

various deeds and documents left in a lawyer's hands. Each of these amounts to an elaborate profession of distrust in those with whom business-transactions have been, or are, or will be, carried on. Clauses are inserted to shut out all possibilities of evasion or perversion, and the whole is so witnessed as to insure that the specified claims and liabilities can be legally proved. Yet all these precautions having been taken, the security supposed to be gained is abandoned. Everything is placed in the legal agent's hands, trusting that he will act honestly; and this notwithstanding the fact that the repute alike of law and of lawyers is not of the highest! Surely a surprising inconsistency!

Many years ago, when on the managing committee of a club, I disgusted the secretary by remarking that in matters of administration, as in matters of business at large, the maxim should be:—Do not suppose things are going right till it is proved they are going wrong, but rather suppose they are going wrong till it is proved they are going right. This was a hard saying for an official to hear; but I hold it to be a saying worthy of recognition by those who are concerned with affairs, private or public. While ignoring this rule of conduct in the many cases where it is most important to follow it, the mass of people follow it tacitly, if not avowedly, in respect of ordinary transactions. What is the meaning of taking a receipt, if not an implied belief in the need for excluding the possibility of going wrong? What are the detailed specifications of every contract and the naming of penalties in case of non-performance? What is the requiring of security when engaging an employé? Or what are the many clauses in an Act of Parliament which are inserted to prevent evasion? These are all recognitions of the truth that things will go wrong unless they are made to go right. And has not every one daily proof of this in the briberies of servants by tradesmen, the illicit commissions of agents, the favouritism shown to certain Government contractors, the purchasing of titled names to strengthen the directing boards of new schemes? Yet in certain spheres confidence continues undiminished and scepticism is reprobated. See for example the history of bank-failures, repeated generation after generation, nearly all resulting from this habit of supposing that things are going right because it has not been shown that they are going wrong. Though managers who have embezzled, directors who have drawn on the funds of the bank for their own uses, and boards who have launched into wild speculations, have time after time shown the proprietaries the need for such measures as shall bring to light misdoings before they have reached great proportions, no safeguards are sought. Almost incredible is the way in which auditors are usually ap-

pointed to banking companies and to companies at
large. Manifestly the institution of an audit was
suggested by the experience that managers or managing bodies could not be implicitly trusted to make
exact statements of the finances, but needed checking by an independent person. The need having
been recognized, one might have supposed that care
would be taken that the check should continue efficient. But we see no care taken. Year after year
reports of company-meetings state that auditors re-
tire but are eligible for re-election, and they are
forthwith re-elected; so that if there should be anything wrong in their own doings, or in their relations with the managing body, there is no likelihood
of disclosure. The truth that for a system of audit to be efficient the auditors should be frequently
changed, passes unregarded. Doubtless inconvenience will be alleged as a reason for not changing;
but inconvenience attends every safeguard. You cannot be insured against fire or accident for nothing;
and you cannot be insured against dishonesty without
paying.

While taught, and professing to believe, that the
human heart is deceitful above all things and desper-
ately wicked, men in cases like these tacitly assume
that the human heart is not at all wicked and is quite
trustworthy. The rational belief lies between these
extremes. It should ever be borne in mind that with

a type of human nature such as now exists, going wrong is certain to occur in course of time if there are left any openings for going wrong, and that the only prudent course is to be ever seeking out the openings and stopping them up.

SOME REGRETS.

In a paragraph quoted with applause from Mr. Ruskin, I met the statement that " all other efforts in education are futile till you have taught your people to love fields, birds, and flowers." Merely noting that in the absence of a predisposition no amount of teaching will produce such a love, I make the obvious remark that life as a whole is not to be included in a love of Nature; and I point the remark by asking what must be thought of Dr. Johnson? Almost devoid though he was of the sense of natural beauty, few will dare to contend that his education was futile. But we have in this assertion one of those multitudinous random exaggerations characterizing Mr. Ruskin's writings.

In reasonable measure the sentiment he expresses is shared in by most people, and by me is shared in very largely. Often when among the Scotch mountains I have pleased myself with the thought that their sides can never be brought under the plough: here at least Nature must ever remain unsubdued. Though subordination to human wants is sometimes suggested by the faint tinklings of distant sheepbells, or by some deer on the sky-line, yet these do not deduct from, but rather add to, the poetry of the scene. In such places one may forget for a while the prosaic aspects of civilization.

I detest that conception of social progress which presents as its aim, increase of population, growth of wealth, spread of commerce. In the politico-economic ideal of human existence there is contemplated quantity only and not quality. Instead of an immense amount of life of low type I would far sooner see half the amount of life of a high type. A prosperity which is exhibited in Board-of-Trade tables year by year increasing their totals, is to a large extent not a prosperity but an adversity. Increase in the swarms of people whose existence is subordinated to material development is rather to be lamented than to be rejoiced over. We assume that our form of social life under which, speaking generally, men toil to-day that they may gain the means of toiling to-morrow, is a satisfactory form, and profess ourselves anxious to spread it all over the world; while we speak with reprobation of the relatively easy and contented lives passed by many of the peoples we call uncivilized. But the ideal we cherish is a transitory one—appropriate, perhaps, to a phase of human development during which the passing generations are sacrificed in the process of making easier the lives of future generations. Intrinsically, a state in which our advance is measured by spread of manufactures and a concomitant production of such regions as the "Black Country," looking as though it had lately been invaded by an army of chimney-sweeps, is a state to be emerged from as quickly as may be. It is a state which in sundry respects compares ill with the past, and is far from that which we may hope will be attained in the future.

One of its evil results is the threatened submergence of those still-remaining traces of a life which, though ruder and simpler, left men some leisure in which to live.

This over-running of the old by the new strikes me afresh with every summer's sojourn in the country, and deepens my regret. An American lady, after staying for some time in England, expressed to me the opinion that a country without ruined castles and abbeys is not worth living in. I fully understood her feeling and to a considerable extent sympathized with her. Though intensely modern and having but small respect for ancient ideas and institutions, I have great pleasure in contemplating the remains bequeathed by the times that are gone. Not that the interest is in any degree an historical one. A guide who begins his daily repeated series of facts or fictions about the ancient place he is showing me over, quickly has his story cut short. I do not care to be distracted by it from the impression of antiquity and

from enjoyment of the half-hidden beauties of the old
walls and arches made more picturesque by decay.
And so is it with the old rural life that is rapidly
passing away as towns and town-habits and town-
ideas invade the country.

As in numerous parts of the Earth appropriated
by us the native races are being " improved " out of
existence, so at home the progress of " improvement "
is yearly leaving less and less of the things which
made the country attractive. Under the western end
of the South Downs, where I have taken up my abode
this season, daily drives show me beauties future generations will not see. The vast hedges overrun with
clematis, and bryony, and wild hop, occupying as
they do great breadths and casting wide shadows, are
not tolerated by the advanced agriculturist. It is the
same with the broad strips of greensward and wild
flowers bordering the by-roads, no less than with the
tortuous lanes, such as those around Woolbeding and
Iping, where the track, deep down below the surface,
is over-arched by foliage here and there pierced by
sun-gleams. All of them seem fated to go, and to
leave only post-and-rail or wire fences, or dwarf,
closely-cropped hedges. The cottage roofs of thatch
are being everywhere replaced by slate or tile roofs;
and there is a gradual disappearance of half-wooden
houses. Another trait of the country, familiar in my
early days, is disappearing. Where a brook crossed
2

the road, a couple of planks and a handrail served to carry over pedestrians, while horses, carts, and carriages had to go through the water: an inconvenience only in times of flood. But now County Councils with members severally anxious to gain popularity by proposing something which "gives work," will soon replace all these by brick or stone bridges. Only here and there, where a path through the fields is carried over a small stream by a foot-bridge, will it still be possible to lean over the handrail and watch the minnows as they slowly come out of their hiding-places into which your shadow had frightened them.

Various usages, too, which as seen in recollection are picturesque, are disappearing. Nowadays it is a rare thing to find gleaners; and in many parts of the country the gathering of mushrooms is forbidden. No longer when passing a barn on a winter's day may one hear the alternating thuds of the flails, and no longer may one be awakened on a bright morning in June by the sharpening of scythes—a sound so disagreeable in itself but made so delightful by its associations.

While in some respects we may envy posterity, we may in one respect pity them. This disappearance of remnants and traces of earlier forms of life, intrinsically picturesque as well as picturesque by association, will deprive them of much poetry which now relieves the prose of life. Everywhere it is the same.

Egypt, made like Europe by railways, steamboats, and hotels scattered along the Nile, will soon cease to excite the feelings proper to its antiquity. Modernized Rome is losing all likeness to Rome as it was even fifty years ago. And here around us the romance of the past is being extinguished by the dull realities of the present. Of course we shall bequeath many remains of existing civilization; but it may well be doubted whether they will be as interesting as those which old times have bequeathed to us.

A PROBLEM.

PEOPLE devoid of musical perceptions have some compensations: one of them being that they are not persecuted by tunes which have obtained lodgments in consciousness and cannot for a time be expelled. Most if not all who have ordinarily good ears are liable to be annoyed by these invading melodies— often those vulgar ones originating in music-halls and everywhere repeated by street-pianos. One remedy for the evil, which is temporarily if not permanently efficient, is that of voluntarily taking up in thought some other melody: the result being that as consciousness will not contain both, the original intruder is for a time extruded. There is some danger, however, that the invited occupant will get possession instead. This, however, by the way.

My reason for referring to this annoyance is that the associated facts throw a side-light on the dispute concerning the *Ego*. Metaphysical discussions often postulate the innate knowledge of a distinct, coherent, ever-present personality. With some it is an axiom that along with the consciousness of objective existence there is indissolubly joined the consciousness of subjective existence—the idea of Self is inseparable from the idea of not-Self. This dogma appears at first sight unassailable. But when the consciousness of Self is critically examined, difficulties present themselves; and, among them, difficulties of the class I have just exemplified. For it is not always possible to say of certain portions of consciousness whether they are to be included in the *Ego* or not. In the instance named the reason for doubt is conspicuous; and it is especially conspicuous when, as in my own case and in the cases of others I have cross-questioned, the intruding melody persists during sleep. Repeatedly I have observed on awaking that it was the first thing of which I was conscious. What then is the mode of existence of this organized set of tones, so coherent that when partly repeated it insists on completing itself, and then after an instant recommences? In what way does this rebellious portion of consciousness stand related to the rest? We can hardly include it in what we call the *Ego*, seeing that the *Ego* continually tries to repress it and fails. And yet if it is not a part of the *Ego*, what is it?

There are numerous facts of kindred nature. When I look at my hand the impression received unquestionably forms part of my consciousness— whether to be considered as a passing phase of the *Ego* itself, or as an effect wrought on it, is a question we may leave undiscussed. But now near the margin

of the large visual area which takes in multitudinous
objects in the room, there is on the one side a vague
impression of the fireplace, of which I may or may
not think, and on the other side, of the window, the
idea of which as a window may or may not enter my
mind. There is also an outermost fringe of the visual
area from which there come to me impressions that
are meaningless unless I turn my eyes towards their
source: even if I think of them I cannot, without
moving, tell their natures. In what relations, then,
do these various indefinite impressions stand to the
Ego? I cannot even say that they form parts of consciousness in the ordinary sense, since, while observing things immediately before me, I am scarcely
aware that these remote ones are there, though they
are unquestionably included in the aggregate filling
my mental field. Still less can I say how these vague
outliers stand related to that part of consciousness
which I regard as my mental Self. Like questions
may be raised respecting the desires and emotions,
faint or strong, which often continue to intrude spite
of endeavours to keep them out; and which thus
seem to be modes of consciousness in antagonism with
the consciousness thought of as constituting the *Ego*.

But the most distinct and striking example of this
detached antagonistic portion of consciousness is that
with which I set out—the invading melody. For its
tones form an organized and integrated cluster of

states of consciousness quite independent of such part of consciousness as I call myself, and which is in conflict with it and continually triumphs over it.

From the physio-psychological point of view the interpretation of this phenomenon is not difficult; but how the pure metaphysician is to solve it I cannot see.

A FEW AMERICANISMS.

WHEN to protest against new words or new uses of old words, and when to accept them, is not easy to decide. If purists had ruled from the beginning, language would never have progressed. Without hesitation, however, we may condemn perversions of words, and may frown on the pedantry which adopts long words where short ones would be as good or better.

Some misapplications of words that are common in America have often vexed me—one especially, the use of the word " claim " instead of " say " or " assert " or " affirm " or " allege "; e. g.—" I claim that he knew all about it before he laid the bet." This abuse has of late, I am sorry to say, made its appearance in English journals of repute, even in *The Times*. A monthly magazine furnishes me with a double example. An English critic and the American writer he criticizes, both pervert the word in the space of three sentences. Speaking of the Cubans the one says:—" The claim that they are not capable of governing themselves has not been established in the writer's experience "; and the other says:—" It is not intended in this description of affairs to claim

16

that the Cubans are without faults." This misuse is
inexcusable because there are sundry words serving
rightly to express the intended meaning, while the
word employed does not express it. A thing claimed
is a thing which may be possessed; but one who
claims that A behaved better than B, implies possession in no sense either actual or potential.

Business men in America often commit another
linguistic outrage—not indeed of the same kind but
of a kind to be strongly reprobated. Here are examples. " The company have leased the new line and
will *operate* it." " The cost of *operating* the factory
has been so-and-so." Everywhere these words replace
the words " work " and " working "—words which,
though open to objection, have not the vice of mere
pedantry. And now this abuse, too, is creeping in
here. I have just met with the sentence:—" Auto-
matic couplers can be operated with ease."

A corruption no less reprehensible, common in
American speech, is the use of " on " in place of
" in ":—" I met him *on* Broadway "; " I found him
on the cars." Here we have a deliberate abolition
of a convenient distinction which in good English
is uniformly observed. The word " in " implies inclosure more or less decided—" in a box," " in a carriage." The word " on " negatives inclosure—implies that the object is not shut up, and, further, that
there are no restraining boundaries near it. The dis-

tinction is marked with precision in two such phrases
as—" in a field " and " on a common ": the circumstances being in all respects alike save in the presence
of inclosing fences in the one case and their absence
in the other case. The disuse of this convenient distinction is a retrograde step, for development of language, as of thought, is a progress in establishing dis-
criminations—a making of existing words more precise
and introducing others to mark further differences.

Men ought to regard their language as an in-
heritance to be conserved, and improved so far as that
is possible, and ought not to degrade it by reversion
to lower types. It should be a matter of conscience
not to misuse words; it should also be a matter of
conscience to resist misuse of them. Especially
should our own language be thus guarded. If, as
several unbiassed foreign judges hold, the English
language will be, and ought to be, the universal language, it becomes the more a duty to mankind to
check bad habits of speech.

Perhaps a little might be done if in return for
criticisms on Americanisms like those above passed,
Americans were systematically to expose deteriora-
tions in the language as spoken here. They might,
for example, mercilessly ridicule that vulgar misuse
of the word " awfully " which has now continued for
more than a generation. There is plenty of scope for
denouncing of kindred perversions.

PRESENCE OF MIND.

WHILE most faculties admit of increase by education, there are some universally recognized as innate, and but little capable of change. We may include Presence of Mind among these. Still, by certain disciplines a great faculty of this kind may be made greater and a small one may be to some degree augmented.

A generation ago the autobiography of a well-known conjurer or *prestidigitateur*—it may have been Houdin—contained an instructive passage, quoted in a review which I saw. It was to the effect that sometimes the autobiographer and his son, when going along a street, competed with one another in naming all the objects they saw in a shop-window while passing it—an intentional exercise of the ability to perceive many things at a glance. A high degree of such an ability was obviously needful for one who deluded others by his sleight-of-hand tricks. Might not the power of rapid and complete observation be increased in children by devices nearly akin to games? Suppose a blackboard in front of which can be drawn at a variable speed a black linen screen, containing a

square opening through which marks on the board are
visible for a moment while the opening passes them.
The teacher might begin with, say, three conspicuous
spots irregularly placed on the board while standing
with his back to the class so as to hide them.   Then,
having drawn the opaque part of the screen across
them, he, when his pupils are ready, lets a spring pull
back the screen so that these spots become visible,
say for a second or two seconds; and the pupils thereupon place dots on their slates as nearly as they can
in like relative positions: comparisons presently
showing which has approached nearest to the original.
The relative positions of the spots may of course be
varied in any way, and their number may be increased
one at a time, to four, five, six.   Three lines may
next be taken, unlike in their lengths, directions, and
relative positions, and analogous complications may
follow.   Thence the transition may be to figures: say
a triangle, a circle, and a straight line, variously
placed with regard to one another; and so on
through higher combinations: the length of the ex-
posure being decreased as the power of rapid perception becomes greater.   More useful, however, because
more interesting, are exercises of this nature yielded
by indoor games—some of those played by children
and some of those played by young people.   There
are card-games success in which depends on quickly
seeing the right place for disposal of a card: all eyes

being turned on each player in turn to detect instantly any error of distribution. Of course while such
lessons and games increase the observational powers
of all, they leave to the last great differences among
them. These are entailed by the physiological limit
implied by what astronomers and others call " the
personal equation." Between the instant when a certain thing is seen and the making of a mark or signal,
there is an interval which is greater in one person
than in another: the cause being that the speed of
the nervous discharge varies. Of course the number
of things observable at once is governed by this. It
should be added that apart from the advantage gained
by greater quickness of perception there is the more
general advantage of raised intensity of attention.
On the ability to concentrate the intellectual powers
upon anything before them, success of many kinds
depends.

But now supposing presence of mind is to some
extent made greater by increasing the ability to see
instantly all the circumstances of a case, there remains to be increased the equally important factor—
fertility of resource. Here little can be done. Possibly by questions asked à propos of an imagined disaster, to be answered in, say, five seconds, some exercise might be given to the appropriate powers of
thought which ordinarily are never exercised. A
lady has set her dress on fire:—what would you do?

" Run for water," would be one answer. " Fetch a
blanket and wrap it round her," might be another.
" Tear down the window curtain if it is woollen, and
roll her in it," might be a third. And perhaps a
fourth would be—" Pull her down backwards and
put the hearth-rug over her." Again, suppose a runaway horse, no longer controllable by the driver:—
what shall be done? " Jump out," will in some cases
be suggested. Another might say—" If the road is
not full of vehicles let the horse gallop till he is
tired." And a third answer may be—" Lie down in
the bottom of the carriage." Once more imagine
you are endeavouring to save a man who is drown-
ing:—how will you proceed? One reply is—" Give
him a hand and swim with the free arm." Another
may say—" Seize him by the collar and use the other
arm for swimming." And a third suggestion will be
—" Get behind his back to avoid grappling and push
him before you as you swim." In each case the subsequent conversation would disclose reasons why
some methods were bad, others better, and another
the best. Naturally the incidents of life furnish
numerous kindred problems, and the ability quickly
to hit on the best course to be followed may to some
slight extent be augmented. At the same time repeated exercises of this kind will stock the memory
with ways of proceeding which may serve when actual accidents occur.

But as there is a constitutional limit to acquirement of quickness of observation, so there is a constitutional limit to acquirement of that resourceful
faculty needed to meet emergencies. The normal
working of an animal organism, human or other, implies that the part or parts called on to perform extra
duty shall immediately be supplied with extra blood:
a muscle at rest suddenly excited to action must
forthwith have its arteries better filled, and the stom-
ach after food has been taken must have its blood-
vessels more fully charged than when it is doing nothing. So with the brain. To yield the quick and vivid
thought and feeling required for coping with disaster,
actual or impending, the cerebral circulation must be
exalted, and by a well-toned vascular system this need
is fulfilled. But here comes in a frequent interference. Fainting as a result of violent emotion is a
common experience. We see in it one of those auto-
matic arrangements for warding off organic disasters
of which there are many. For violent emotion implies that parts of the brain have suddenly become
surcharged with blood: a concomitant being that
some of the over-distended arterioles are in danger
of giving way under the pressure—a mischief which
must be serious and may be fatal. Under these conditions there comes into play, through the action of
the vagus-nerve, a sudden reining in of the heart: it
ceases to act and the pressure on the blood-vessels,

thereupon diminished, ceases to be dangerous. But now between the ordinary mental state accompanying the ordinary cerebral circulation, and this extreme state in which arrest of mental action results from arrest of cerebral circulation, there are all gradations; that is, there are all degrees in the reining in of the heart, short of absolute arrest. But from diminished heart-power it results that instead of the appropriate exaltation of mental force there is a greater or less decrease of it. The needful supply of blood to the whole of the brain being partially withheld, the faculties are partially thrown out of gear. The thoughts become confused and there is something like a temporary paralysis of intellect. Especially does this happen in nervous subjects and those who, by over-stress, have permanently injured the vascular system and the nervous centres. In such this failure of blood-supply in presence of a danger or catastrophe, physical or moral, produces something like a mental chaos—a derangement of ideas and impulses such that everything goes wrong, and either nothing is done or something just opposite to that which should be done.

Depending thus in chief measure on constitution, natural or modified by disorder, presence of mind cannot be much increased by culture. Still something may be done. Practice in rapidity of observation and fertility of resource must benefit all, whatever natures they may have; and where emergencies are not of an alarming kind may increase the presence of mind even of the nervous. Though little is to be expected it is well to attempt that little. Remembering that occasionally presence of mind means salvation to self or others from evils that are serious, if not fatal, it will be inferred that discipline or exercise tending even in a small degree to make it greater, might fitly take the place of many worthless lessons which form large parts of current education.

THE CORRUPTION OF MUSIC.

Music-performers and teachers of music are corrupters of music. This is a paradox most people will think extremely absurd. I am about to justify it.

Without going back for proof to past days, when from time to time a prima donna forced a composer to introduce passages enabling her to display her vocal agility, I will limit myself to the present. Justifications meet me continually. Here, for instance, is an extract from a recent musical criticism, in which, after remarking that the sonata in question is not a good one, the writer goes on—

"It is not difficult to understand the attraction which this work possesses for first-rate pianists; there are difficulties in it to be conquered."

And here is another:—

"Miss ——'s vocal method is not beyond criticism, but as she succeeds in emitting sounds at a height not usually attained, the public is quite satisfied."

Hamlet, in his address to the players, reprobated those who "split the ears of the groundlings who, for the most part, are capable of nothing but inexplicable dumb shows and noise." Changing time, place, and terms, it may be said that three-fourths of musical audiences at the present day are in the same relative position. They appreciate but little the musical ideas and feelings of the composer, or the effective rending of them; but an extraordinary feat of vocalization, or a display of marvellous gymnastics on the violin, brings a round of applause. And then, unhappily, as the members of the orchestra applaud—applaud because they know how great are the difficulties overcome—the audience is encouraged in the belief that this is music, and clap lest they should be thought persons of no taste. In this way performers, desiring less to render faithfully the meanings of the pieces they play than to exhibit their powers of execution, vitiate the music and the tastes of their hearers. Direct evidence has come to me from two lady-pianists, both of whom played at concerts pieces which they chose not because they were beautiful but because they were of kinds making it possible to show brilliancy of performance: a *toccata* was the programme-name of one. The elder of these ladies, who was a teacher of music, admitted that she hoped to show parents what a good teacher she must be to be able to play in that style!

As is implied by these confessions, the mischief originates in the performer's pre-occupation with self, for this largely excludes occupation with the composer's thoughts. The dominant feeling is not love of the music rendered but desire for the applause which brilliant rendering will bring. In the cases of celebrated performers to whom crowds of hearers flock, this is almost a necessity. Many years ago, when coming away from a concert given by a celebrated Russian pianist, I remarked—"Too little music and too much Rubinstein."

Nor is this all. There is a more widely diffused and less obtrusive mischief. A dominant trait of brilliant musical execution is rapidity. A *Saltarello* or a *Tarantelle* is easy enough, provided it be played slowly. The skill is shown in playing it with great speed; and teachers incite their pupils to achieve this great speed. The result is gradually to raise the standard of time, and the conception of what is the appropriate time is everywhere being changed in the direction of acceleration. This affects not pieces of display only but pieces of genuine music. So much is this the case that habitually when ladies have played to me I have had to check them—"Not so fast, not so fast!" the rate chosen being usually such as to destroy the sentiment.

In brief, this vitiation is one of the indirect results of the aim on the part of professionals not to render most perfectly the ideas of the composer, but so to play as to increase their own earnings.

SPONTANEOUS REFORM.

ELSEWHERE I have illustrated the curious truth that while an evil is very great it attracts little or no attention; that when, from one or other cause, it is mitigated, recognition of it brings efforts to decrease it; and that when it has much diminished, there comes a demand that strong measures shall be taken for its extinction: natural means having done so much, a peremptory call for artificial means arises.

One of the instances I named was the immense decline in drunkenness which has taken place since the 18th century, followed, during recent times, by a loud advocacy of legislation for suppressing it. The occasion for recalling this instance has been the discovery of some evidence showing how extreme were the excesses of our great-great-grandfathers. In one of a series of diocesan histories on the shelves of a country house, I found some extracts from the diary of a Thomas Turner, a mercer, &c. in a Sussex village. His entries show him to have been a reader of good literature and a religious man. The compiler says of him—

"When he has not got too drunk on Saturday evenings he goes to church on Sunday. He always makes some criticism

on the sermon . . . Bad as he was, however, in regard to in-
temperance, he does not seem to have been much worse than
most of his neighbours. Whether they met for business or for
pleasure " the ordinary result was that " the company broke up
in a state of intoxication."

Here are some of Mr. Turner's confessions:—

"April 21, 1756. Went to the audit, and came home
drunk . . . Nov. 25. The curate of Laughton came to the
shop . . . and also stayed in the afternoon till he got in liquor,
and being so complaisant as to keep him company I was quite
drunk. A party of 15 people, including the vicar of the parish,
Mr. Porter, and his wife, meet at four in the afternoon. After
supper . . . ' drinking all the time as fast as it could be well
poured down.' About three o'clock in the morning he manages
to get home ' without even tumbling.' His wife is brought
back two hours later." And then, at the instigation of Mrs.
Porter, the vicar's wife, the carouse is resumed next morning.
On Sunday " ' we had as good a sermon as I ever heard Mr.
Porter preach, it being against swearing.' " Only a few
days afterwards the same party of people met at Mr. Porter's.
" ' We continued,' he says, ' drinking like horses, and singing
till many of us were very drunk.' "

One further extract shows in an instructive manner
the social sanction, or something more, which these
usages had. Making note of an invitation he has received, the diarist writes:—

" ' If I go I must drink just as they please, or otherwise I
shall be called a poor, singular fellow. If I stay at home I
shall be stigmatized with the name of being a poor, proud, ill-
natured wretch.' . . . So he resolves to go . . . ' Before I
came away I think I may say there was not one sober person
in the company.' "

Another diarist, a Mr. Walter Gane, schoolmaster,
makes similar confessions; and other details given

show that throughout society at large this demoralization everywhere ran. Credibility is thus given to a passage contained in the *Tour to the Hebrides*, which, in the absence of this verifying evidence, would seem incredible.

"Dr. Johnson observed that our drinking less than our ancestors was owing to the change from ale to wine. 'I remember,' said he, 'when all the *decent* people in Lichfield got drunk every night, and were not the worse thought of.'"

Largely as we may discount this statement, we must conclude that the general inebriety was astoundingly great.

What has produced the transformation which has since taken place? Not legislation, not stern repression, not coercion. The improvement has slowly arisen, along with other social improvements, from natural causes. The *vis medicatrix naturæ* has been in operation. But this large fact and other large facts having like implications are ignored by our agitators. They cannot be made to recognize the process of evolution resulting from men's daily activities, though facts forced on them from morning till night show this in myriadfold ways. The houses they live in, their furniture, clothes, fuel, food—all are brought into existence by the spontaneous efforts of citizens supplying one another's wants. The pastures and cornfields they travel through, cover areas originally moor and bog, which have been transformed by individual enterprise. The roads, the railways, the

trains, the telegraphs, are products of combined exertions prompted by desires for profit and maintenance. The villages and towns they pass exhibit the
accretions due to private actions. The districts devoted to one or other manufacture have been so devoted by men who were simply seeking incomes to
live upon. The enormous distributing organization
with its vast warehouses and retail shops lining the
streets, carrying everywhere innumerable kinds of
commodities, has arisen without the planning of anyone. Market towns, large and small, have without
forethought become places of periodic exchanges;
while exchanges of higher and larger kinds have established themselves in London, where, from hour to
hour, you may feel the pulse of the world. So, too, by
spontaneous co-operation has grown up that immense
mercantile marine, sailing and steaming, which takes
men everywhere and brings goods from all places.
And no less are we indebted to the united doings of
private individuals for that network of submarine
telegraphs by which there is now established something like a universal consciousness. All these things
are non-governmental. If we ask how arose the science which guided the development of them, we find
its origin to have been non-governmental. If we ask
whence came all the multitudinous implied inven-
tions, the reply is that their origin, too, was non-governmental. Of the Press, daily, weekly, monthly,

we still have to say it is non-governmental. It is so with the great torrent of books continually issuing, as well as with the arts—music, painting, sculpture, in their various developments—and with the amusements, filling hours of relaxation. This vast social organization, the life of which we severally aid and which makes our lives possible by satisfying our wants, is just as much a naturally-developed product as is the language by which the wants are communicated. No State-authority, no king or council, made the one any more than the other. The ridiculous Carlylean theory of the Great Man and his achievements, absolutely ignores this genesis of social structures and functions which has been going on through the ages. The deeds of the ruler who modifies the actions of his generation, it confounds with the evolution of the great body-politic itself, of which those actions are but incidents. It is as though a child, seeing for the first time a tree from which a gardener is here cutting off a branch and there pruning away smaller parts, should regard the gardener, the only visible agent, as the creator of the whole structure: knowing nothing about the agency of sun and rain, air and soil. Undeveloped intelligences cannot recognize the results of slow, silent, invisible causes.

Education and culture as we now see them, do nothing to diminish this incapacity but tend rather to

increase it. In so far as they are more than linguistic, the "Humanities," to which the attention of
the young is mainly given, are concerned with per-
sonalities. After the traditional doings of gods and
heroes, of great leaders and their conquests, come the
products of the poets, of the historians, of the phi-
losophers. And when study of earlier ages is supple-
mented by study of later ages, we find the so-called
history composed of kings' biographies, the narratives
of their conflicts, the squabbles and intrigues of their
vassals and dependents. In the consciousness of one
who has passed through the *curriculum* universally
prevailing until recently, there is no place for natural
causation. Instead, there exists only the thought of
what, in a relative sense, is artificial causation—the
causation by appointed agencies and through force
directed by this or that individual will. Small
changes wrought by officials are clearly conceived,
but there is no conception of those vast changes which
have been wrought through the daily process of
things undirected by authority. And thus the notion
that a society is a manufacture and not an evolution,
vitiates political thinking at large; leading, as in the
case which has served me for a text, to the belief that
only by coercion can benefits be achieved. Is an evil
shown? then it must be suppressed by law. Is a good
thing suggested? then let it be compassed by an Act
of Parliament.

FEELING *VERSUS* INTELLECT.

In the early days of my friendship with Prof. Huxley—I think about 1854—an afternoon call on him quickly brought the suggestion—" Come upstairs; I want to show you something which will delight you—a fact that goes slick through a great generalization! " His ironical expression was prompted by his consciousness that being so much given to generalizing I should be disconcerted. He was dissecting the brain of a porpoise, and the anomalous fact he pointed out was that the porpoise has a brain of relatively immense size—a size seemingly out of all relation to the creature's needs. What can an animal leading so simple a life want with an organ almost large enough to carry on the life of a human being? Huxley (not then professor) had no solution of the difficulty to offer, and at the time there did not occur to me what I believe to be the solution.

There has grown up universally an identification of mind with intelligence. Partly because the guidance of our actions by thought is so conspicuous, and partly because speech, which occupies so large a space in our lives, is a vehicle that makes thought pre-

dominant to ourselves and others, we are led to suppose that the thought-element of mind is its chief element: an element often excluding from recognition
every other.   Consequently, when it is said that the
brain is the organ of the mind, it is assumed that the
brain is chiefly if not wholly the organ of the intellect.

The error is an enormous one.   The chief component of mind is feeling.   To see this it is necessary
to get rid of the wrong connotations which the word
mind has acquired, and to use instead its equivalent
—consciousness.   Mind properly interpreted is co-ex-
tensive with consciousness: all parts of consciousness
are parts of mind.   Sensations and emotions are parts
of consciousness, and so far from being its minor
components they are its major components.   In the
first place the mass of consciousness at any moment
consists of the sensations produced in us by things
around — the various assemblages of colours impressed through our eyes, the sounds which salute
our ears, the pressures on parts of our bodies as we
lie, sit, or stand, the muscular strains accompanying
our movements, and occasionally tastes and odours.
Among these numerous peripheral feelings there is
every instant an establishment of relations constituting perceptions and thoughts—colours occupying
certain areas and positions are recognized as such and
such things by assimilation to ideal sets of colours

similarly arranged, and from the movements of certain groups of them particular results are foreseen: these foreseen results being ideal groups of feelings. And so with all the sounds, touches, odours, warmths: the intellectual element being limited to recognition of the co-existences and sequences among these. So that the *body* even of our thought-consciousness consists of feelings, and only the *form* constitutes what we distinguish as intelligence: there is no intelligence in a sensation of red, or of sweetness, or of hardness, or of effort, but only in certain co-ordinations of such sensations.

And then comes the other great class of feelings, ignored in the current conception of mind—the emotions. Of these, as of the sensations, it is observable that the ordinary ones present from moment to moment are not regarded as feelings at all. Like respirations or winkings of the eyes, their unceasingness makes us oblivious of them. Yet every instant emotions are present. No movement is made but what is preceded by a prompting feeling as well as a prompting thought. And it needs only that the movement shall be large, or difficult, or resisted, to make us aware that an emotion of some kind was its antecedent. So is it with all the other feeble emotions. The day is fine, and there is a slight exaltation of mental state. It is rainy, and a comparative dulness results. Some one liked comes in, and a wave

of agreeable consciousness arises; while an emotional
cloud follows the sight of an enemy. Similarly with
occupations.   There is some task-work to be done,
and behind all the bodily and mental activities needed, there lies a dim feeling of aversion—a feeling differing greatly from that which accompanies the working at a hobby or the achievement of a success. And
then though the aggregate feeling ever passing is so
unobtrusive that we hardly think of it as existing,
it becomes, under exciting circumstances, almost the
sole occupant of consciousness. If altercation rouses
extreme anger, the emotion may become so great as
even to exclude the power of speech: the thought-
element is overwhelmed.   Intense alarm may so
throw the intellect out of gear as to produce temporary inability to act. The anxiety bred of absorbing
affection may extinguish all irrelevant ideas.   And
this mental element which thus upon occasion shows
itself supreme, is in a sense supreme at all times; for
the prevailing emotions, higher or lower, are those
components of mind which determine the daily conduct, now dutiful now lax, now noble now base. That
part which we ordinarily ignore when speaking of
mind is its essential part. The emotions are the masters, the intellect is the servant. The guidance of our
acts through perception and reason has for its end
the satisfaction of feelings, which at once prompt the
acts and yield the energy for performance of the acts;

for all the exertions daily gone through, whether accompanied by agreeable or disagreeable feelings, are gone through that certain other feelings may be obtained or avoided.

Here, then, is the solution of the anomaly named at the outset. The large brain of the porpoise is not the agent of much intellectual activity, but it is the agent of much emotional activity, accompanying the pursuit and capture of prey. That enormous muscular power exhibited by the creature—exhibited sometimes in its superfluous gambols while keeping up with a swift vessel—is the expression of an enormous outflow of feeling; for without the correlative feeling there could not be the muscular contraction. It is in generating this great body of feeling and concomitant energy, perpetually expended in the movements of the chase, that its brain is mainly occupied.

The multiplication of effects, which is a universal trait in the cosmic process, is well illustrated by the way in which errors ramify and eventually influence multitudinous things they are seemingly unconcerned with. That I might indicate some perverted conceptions arising from it, has been my purpose in pointing out this immense mistake commonly made in identifying mind with intellect.

For in these days, when it is assumed that, as components of the human being, mind and body stand the one high above the other (if indeed we can say this in presence of athleticism, and the giving of greater honour to the stroke of a winning eight than to a senior wrangler)—in these days when theoretically if not practically the mental dominates over the physical, grave evil arises from leaving the more important part of the mental out of account. The over-valuation of intelligence necessarily has for its concomitant under-valuation of the emotional nature. Considered in respect of their fitness for life, individual and social, those in whom the altruistic sentiments predominate are far superior to those who, with powers of perception and reasoning of the highest kinds join anti-social feelings —unscrupulous egoism and disregard of fellow-men. The contrast between some uncivilized tribes well illustrates this truth. Among savages the Fijians were, when found, remarkable for their cleverness, and for an ability to think which the lower races rarely show; while at the same time cannibalism was rampant among them, slave-tribes were preserved for food, and it was an ambition to be a known murderer. On the other hand the peaceful Arafuras are not described as intelligent: some of their ideas imply the contrary. But living together as they do without antagonisms and with only nominal government, their feelings are such that one who, being young, was disappointed in his desire to be chief (a distinction mainly implying responsibility for the welfare of poorer tribesmen) consoled himself by saying—" Well, I can still use my property in helping my fellows." When thus put in apposition, the superiority of the moral element to the intellectual element becomes conspicuous. So long as it will hold together, a society wicked in the extreme may be formed of men who in keenness of intellect rank with Mephistopheles; and, conversely, though its members are stupid and unprogressive, a society may be full of happiness if its members are scrupulously regardful of one another's claims, and actively sympathetic. This proposition, though almost a truism, is little regarded. Full recognition of its truth would make men honour, much more than they do, the unobtrusively good, and think less of those whose merit is intellectual ability. There would, for example, be none of the unceasing admiration for that transcendent criminal, Napoleon.

An over-valuation of teaching is necessarily a concomitant of this erroneous interpretation of mind. Everywhere the cry is—Educate, educate, educate! Everywhere the belief is that by such culture as schools furnish, children, and therefore adults, can be moulded into the desired shapes. It is assumed that when men are taught what is right, they will do what is right—that a proposition intellectually accepted will be morally operative. And yet this conviction, contradicted by every-day experience, is at

4

variance with an every-day axiom—the axiom that
each faculty is strengthened by exercise of it—intellectual power by intellectual action, and moral
power by moral action.   The current notion is that
these causes and effects can be transposed—that assent to an injunction will be followed by exercise of
the correlative feeling.   It is true that where the
feeling is already active, or the capacity for it exists,
some effect may result; but where the feeling is dormant or congenitally deficient, the injunction practically does nothing: unless, indeed, it excites repug-
nance, as sometimes happens.   It seems, however,
that this unlimited faith in teaching is not to be
changed by facts.   Though in presence of multitudinous schools, high and low, we have the rowdies and
Hooligans, the savage disturbers of meetings, the
adulterators of food, the givers of bribes and receiv-
ers of corrupt commissions, the fraudulent solicitors,
the bubble companies, yet the current belief continues unweakened; and recently in America an outcry
respecting the yearly increase of crime, was joined
with an avowed determination not to draw any inference adverse to their educational system.   But the
refusal to recognize the futility of mere instruction
as a means to moralization, is most strikingly shown
by ignoring the conspicuous fact that after two
thousand years of Christian exhortations, uttered
by a hundred thousand priests throughout Europe,

pagan ideas and sentiments remain rampant, from emperors down to tramps. Principles admitted in theory are scorned in practice. Forgiveness is voted dishonourable. An insult must be wiped out by blood: the obligation being so peremptory that an officer is expelled the army for even daring to question it. And in international affairs the sacred duty of revenge, supreme with the savage, is supreme also with the so-called civilized.

As implied above, this undue faith in teaching is mainly caused by the erroneous conception of mind. Were it fully understood that the emotions are the masters and the intellect the servant, it would be seen that little can be done by improving the servant while the masters remain unimproved. Improving the servant does but give the masters more power of achieving their ends.

THE PURPOSE OF ART.

The educational mania, having for its catchwords "Enlightenment, Information, Instruction," tends in all ways to emphasize this erroneous indentification of mind with intellect; and consequently affects the estimates men make of various mental activities and mental products. Among other results it vitiates their conceptions of Art and the purpose of Art: using the word Art in the sense now generally accepted as comprehensive of all works of creative imagination. In this sphere, as in other spheres, there is under-valuation of the emotional element in mind and over-valuation of the intellectual element.

Merely alluding to the unended controversy concerning dramatic art, which has all along turned upon the question whether the stage-representations of life are or are not instructive, as though the production of pleasure were of no account, I may note that in poetry we may see this bringing to the front of thought instead of feeling: instance the dictum of Mr. Matthew Arnold that " it is by a large, free, and sound representation of things, that poetry, *this high criticism of life,* has truth of substance." Not the

44

arousing of certain sentiments but the communication of certain ideas is thus represented as the poet's office.

With pictorial representation the like has happened. Artists seek to magnify their office on the ground that art is useful for intellectual culture: that reason being the only one assigned. Years ago my attention was drawn to this mistaken conception by a disquisition with which Mr. Holman Hunt accompanied an exhibited picture—"Christ in the Workshop," it may have been. The educational value of Art was the theme of his proem. By implication it appeared that it is not enough for a picture to gratify the æsthetic perceptions or raise a pleasurable emotion. It must teach something. The yielding of satisfaction to certain feelings is not regarded as an aim to be put in the foreground, but the primary aim must be instruction. Recently in a lecture delivered before the Ruskin Society of Birmingham by the editor of *The Studio*, I found an expression of the same belief. The words used were:—" The mission of art is to elevate the intelligence and gratify its longings."

And now the same thing is happening in respect of music. This, too, is to be regarded as an intellectual exercise. It is an appeal to mind; and mind being conceived as intellect it is an appeal to intellect. A composer must write to express, not feelings but enlightening ideas, and the listener must seek out and appreciate these ideas. The avowed theory of Wagner was that the purpose of music is to teach. He held certain conceptions of life and considered his operas as vehicles for those conceptions and as agents for propagating them. Some kindred belief is implied by a distinguished disciple over here, who repudiates the supposition that music is to be conceived simply as a source of pleasure. On another side we see a kindred idea. Musical critics often give applause to compositions as being " scientific "—as being meritorious not in respect of the emotions they arouse but as appealing to the cultured intelligence of the musician.

As implied above, I hold these to be perverted beliefs, having their roots in the prevailing enormous error respecting the constitution of mind. In that part of life concerned with music, as in other parts of life, the intellect is the minister and the emotions the things ministered to. Doubtless certain amounts of intellectual perception, implying appropriate culture, are needful for making possible the pleasurable feelings which music is capable of producing. These, however, are but means to an end, and it is a profound mistake to regard them as the end itself. An analogy will help us here. Before there can be sympathy there must have been gained some knowledge of the natural language of the emotions—what tones and changes of voice, what facial expressions, what movements of the body, signify certain states of mind. But the knowledge of this natural language does not constitute sympathy. There may be clear perception of the meanings of all these traits without any production of fellow-feeling. Similarly, then, with the distinction between the knowledge of musical expression in its complex developments, and the experience of those emotions to which the musical expression is instrumental. Only in so far as its cultivated perceptions form a means to that excitement of the feelings which the composer intended to produce, does the intellect properly play a part; and even then, in playing its indispensable part, it is apt to interfere unduly. Many years ago, in the days when I had free admission for two to the Royal Italian Opera, and when, as mentioned in her Life, I frequently took George Eliot as my companion, I remember once remarking to her how much the tendency to analyze the effects we were listening to deducted from the enjoyment of them: my remark calling forth full assent. Consciousness having at any moment but a limited capacity, it results that part of its area cannot be occupied in one way without decreasing the area which can be occupied in another way. The antagonism between intellectual appreciation and emotional satisfaction, is essentially the same as one which lies at the root of our mental structure—the antagonism between sensation and perception; and it runs up throughout the whole content of mind, rising to such partial conflicts between thought and feeling as those which accompany critical judgments of music.

When we come to the alleged higher meaning of music—to that instruction which a composer is assumed to utter and the listener to comprehend, we have yet a further interference with the true end. The intellectual element intrudes still more on the emotional element. In proportion as the listener, instead of being a passive recipient becomes an active interpreter, in that proportion does he lose the kind of consciousness which it is the purpose of the art to produce. If, like Mr. Ernest Newman, he thinks music good in proportion as it " adds something to our knowledge of life " and, while listening, seeks for such knowledge, he will lose that which the music should give him, and, as I believe, will get nothing instead.

Any culture-effect which may rightly be recognized must be consequent on the excitement of the superior emotions. Music may appeal to crude and coarse feelings or to refined and noble ones; and in so far as it does the latter it awakens the higher nature and works an effect, though but a transitory effect, of a beneficial kind. But the primary purpose of music is neither instruction nor culture but pleasure; and this is an all-sufficient purpose.

SOME QUESTIONS.

TETHERED by ill-health to the South of England, I have, since '89, spent the greater part of the summer of each year in a country house—mostly that of some gentleman-farmer whose family and surroundings fulfilled the needful conditions: one being the presence of young people. Taking, in my daily drives, two ladies as companions, and being generally unable to bear continuous conversation, I put a check on this by asking one or other question not to be answered without thought. The practice thus originated became established, and it has since been my habit to set problems, partly by way of gauging the knowledge of young people, and partly by way of exercising their reasoning powers. One of the simplest, which was sometimes answered, is—How happens it that sheep, rabbits, and hares have their eyes on the sides of their heads, while cats and dogs have their eyes nearly in front? Of others, to which the replies are less obvious, and to most of which no answers have been forthcoming, here are a few.

How is it possible for a lark, while soaring, to sing for several minutes without cessation?

What is the reason that in hilly districts the roads

49

Gardner Webb College Library

are deep down below the level of the fields, whereas in flat districts they are on a level with the fields?

Throughout the country, especially in its less frequented parts, the bye-roads, and sometimes even the main roads, have strips of greensward several yards wide on either side of the part used for traffic. In what manner did these strips originate?

Cows and horses drink in the same way that we do, whereas dogs and cats drink by lapping. Whence arises this difference of habit?

Why does a duck waddle in walking? And what is the need for that trait of structure which causes the waddle?

How is it that a bull-dog is able to retain his hold for a longer period than other dogs?

Rookeries are nearly always close to human dwellings, usually of some size. Rooks seem to gain nothing from this proximity, but daily fly far away to their feeding-grounds. Moreover they persist in thus breeding in the trees around houses, though annually many of their young are shot as soon as they can fly. What circumstances have led to this establishment of a home apparently so unfit?

In rambles or drives throughout the country we see few blackbirds or thrushes in the open fields, but we see more as we approach houses, especially good houses, even in parts of the year when there are no temptations from the fruit gardens. Why is this?

In attempted answers to these questions, the noteworthy fact has been the undeveloped idea of causation implied. Not so much that the answers were wrong but that they betrayed no conception of a relevant cause, was the startling revelation. When, for instance, I was asked whether a soaring lark's ability to sing without break is due to the greater purity of the air high up, there was shown entire failure to conceive the physical actions necessitated by a lark's song. Then, again, there were suggested solutions which were utterly indefinite even if relevant. When as a reason why the drinking of cows and horses differs from that of dogs and cats, there came the inquiry—Is it because of some difference in the shapes of their throats? it was clear that had I said Yes, the answer would have been thought sufficient: no conception having been framed of the way in which the suggested difference might account for the unlikeness of habit. Evidently minds left in the implied states are seed-beds for superstitions. That it is unlucky to spill salt, and that the impending ill-luck may be excluded by throwing a pinch over the left shoulder, or that to see the new moon through glass is likely to be followed by some evil, are beliefs accepted without difficulty where there exist no rational ideas of causation. The most absurd dogmas readily find lodgment where no knowledge has been acquired of the order of Nature.

THE ORIGIN OF MUSIC.

FORTY odd years ago I published an essay under the title—" The Origin and Function of Music." The doctrine contained in that essay has been variously criticized, in most cases adversely, both here and abroad. One of the earliest of my critics was Mr. Edmund Gurney, whose reasons for dissent occupied some pages in his work on *The Power of Sound*, as well as an essay in *The Fortnightly Review* for July 1876. To his criticisms I replied in a Postscript some few years ago appended to the original essay (see *Essays*, Library edition, vol. ii, pp. 437–449). In this Postscript I also dealt with the opposed theory of Mr. Darwin, who ascribes human song, as he ascribes the songs of birds, to the incidents of courtship; and have there, I think, shown the untenability of his hypothesis. I propose here to deal with the hypotheses of several others.

In *Mind* for July 1891, Dr. Wallaschek, while combating the view elaborated by me, enunciated the view that the essential element in music is rhythm. He says:—

"It is a well-known fact, established by the observations of travellers and investigators, that the one essential feature in primitive music is rhythm, melody being a matter of accident."

This assertion may, I think, be disposed of in two ways. It is at variance both with the popular conception and with the scientific conception. Observe the popular conception.

Here is a sparrow—the too-familiar sparrow. It sits on the eaves and chirps with tolerable regularity. Especially if it be a young one calling for food, its chirps are regular in their intervals—that is, rhythmical. Here in the adjacent copse is heard a blackbird, uttering successions of notes entirely without rhythm. To which of these kinds of utterance do we apply the word "song"? Not to that of the rhythmical sparrow but to that of the unrhythmical blackbird. And why do we call the utterance of the blackbird a song? Manifestly because it displays the most conspicuous trait of that which we call song in human beings: it is a varying combination of notes differing in pitch. That is to say, we deny the name "song" absolutely to the rhythmical sounds made by the sparrow, in which there is no combination of notes unlike one another, and we give it to the variously-combined sounds made by the blackbird, though these are entirely unrhythmical; and we apply the word "song" to these sounds because they remind us of human song. Unquestionably, then, in the popular conception rhythm is not the essential element in music.

An illustration will best prepare the way for the disproof furnished by analysis. The *Mammalia* are animals which, as the name implies, are characterized by having mammæ—the possession of mammæ essentially characterizes a mammal. "No," might say Dr. Wallaschek, "a mammal's essential characteristic is a vertebral column." In response the naturalist would reply that birds, reptiles, and fishes have also vertebral columns, and that that cannot be the essential trait of a mammal which is a trait possessed by other groups of creatures as well: it must be a trait in which it differs from them. Turn now to the several art-products characterized by rhythm. There are the rhythmical movements constituting the dance. There are the rhythmically-arranged articulations forming verses. And there are the successive vocal sounds of different pitch which compose the chant, in which verses were originally uttered — sounds which may be emitted apart from the words. As these three rhythmical manifestations of feeling were at first simultaneous, rhythm cannot be considered the fundamental element of any one of them rather than of the other two. It belongs to the rhythmical movements and to the rhythmical speech, just as much as to the rhythmical tones. In course of time these manifestations of feeling differentiated: each retaining its rhythm. And that which characterizes any one of the three must be that in which it is unlike the others, not that which it has in common with them.

Thus Dr. Wallaschek's hypothesis ignores entirely the current conception of music and ignores also the principles of scientific classification.

Recently in a clever, and in most respects rational, work, entitled *A Study of Wagner*, Mr. Ernest Newman, with his own adverse arguments, joined those of others. He quoted approvingly the criticism of M. Combarieu:—

"Mr. Spencer neglects or ignores everything that gives to the art he is studying its special and unique character; he does not appear to have realized what a musical composition is." (p. 164.)

Here we have a striking example of the way in which an hypothesis is made to appear untenable by representing it as being something which it does not profess to be. I gave an account of the *origin* of music, and now I am blamed because my conception of the origin of music does not include a conception of music as fully developed! If to someone who said that an oak comes from an acorn it were replied that he had manifestly never seen an oak, since an acorn contains no trace of all its complexities of form and structure, the reply would not be thought a rational one; but it would be quite as rational as this of M. Combarieu, who thinks I have not " realized what a musical composition is " because my theory of the origin of music says nothing about the characteristics of an overture or a quartet. What is every process of evolution but the gradual assumption of traits which were not originally possessed?

Some of Mr. Newman's own criticisms exhibit the same confusion between the origin of a thing and the thing which originates from it. He says:—

"Mr. Spencer himself admits that his theory affords no explanation of the place of harmony in modern music, while many musical æstheticians have found it almost as unsatisfactory in respect to the origin of melody." (p. 163.)

With equal reason the assertion that all mathematics begins with finger-counting might be rejected because, if so, no explanation is forthcoming of the differential calculus! Passing over this, however, let us note two startling corollaries from Mr. Newman's criticism. If a theory of the origin of music is untrue because it does not recognize harmony, then the music of all Oriental peoples is swept away as not being music, since harmony is absent from it. Nay more, early European music, as of the Greeks, consisted solely of single successions of notes constituting melody, or, more strictly, recitative: harmony came into existence only in comparatively modern times. The invalidity of the objection is by these facts made conspicuous. History itself shows us that harmony, being a late development of music, could not possibly be recognized in an account of its origin.

Other passages in Mr. Newman's criticism go far towards conceding that which he denies. He says that—

"vocal music is, broadly speaking, intended to present the verbal sense in another and more intensive form: its function is to re-think the speech-utterance in music. It is evident that this is impossible where the words, having no emotional content," &c.

Surely this is an admission that there is a natural relation between emotions and musical cadences—an admission again made when denying the practicability of giving a musical form to " a purely intellectual utterance." *   In another place, Mr. Newman goes still further towards accepting the view which he sets out to reject.   He writes:—

"Hardly more noticeable is the transition from excited speech to ordinary recitative; the mind feels that it is still in the same atmosphere, though the breathing is a little quickened. But sing a song, or play an adagio upon the piano, and you will realize at once that you have got upon quite a different plane of psychology."   (p. 163.)

To most it will seem strange that along with the belief that there is a natural transition from excited speech to recitative there should go a denial that

---

* Since this was written an amusing illustration has been furnished me by a collection of Handel's "Opera Songs." A song in the opera of *Floridante* commences thus:

" 'Tis worth observing,
   Some must be serving,
   Seeing that we cannot all wear a crown."

5

there can be any such transition from recitative to song.

An illustration will, I think, dispose of this alleged difference in the " plane of psychology." Here is a fabric of simple silk. Here is another fabric, like in colour and quality but figured: the figure, though of the same silk as the ground, being clearly distinguishable from it. Evidently it may be said that the transition from the simple silk to the figured silk, is a transition to something lying in a different plane of construction. Yet the two have a common origin. The Jacquard loom was developed from the ordinary loom, and retains its essential principles: the Jacquard apparatus being superposed on the original apparatus. In like manner, then, such distinction as exists between recitative and melody is a distinction which may be recognized while asserting that the two have a common source: melody rising a step higher than recitative as recitative rises a step higher than excited speech.

Elsewhere, as also in some of the above paragraphs, I have cited direct evidence of development; as instance the fact that the music of Eastern races is not only without harmony but has more the character of recitative than of melody, and the fact that the chant of the Early Greek poet was a recitative with accompaniment in unison on his four-stringed lyre. But Sir Hubert Parry, who adopts the view

I have here re-explained and defended, has in his
chapter on "Folk-Music" exemplified the early
stages of musical evolution, up from the howling
chants of savages—Australians, Caribs, Polynesian
cannibals, &c.—to the rude melodies of our own ancestors. I do not see how any unbiassed reader, after
examining the evidence placed by him in its natural
order, can refuse assent to the conclusion drawn.

The argument may be much strengthened by emphasizing some of the essential points. One of these,
of great significance, I take from an account of
"Omaha Indian Music" by Miss Alice C. Fletcher,
an official of the Ethnological Museum at Cambridge,
Mass. After describing the difficulties she had in
bringing their songs into such forms as we use, she
says:—"I ceased to trouble about theories of scales,
tones, rhythm, and melody "; and then she goes on to
say that she found it difficult to write down the songs
of these Indians because their intervals are so indefinite. Now this is just one of the traits to be expected
if vocal music is developed out of emotional speech;
since the intervals of speech, also, are indefinite. Its
tones have no such sharp and fixed distinctions as
those by which the notes of song are characterized.
A higher stage of the transition is strikingly shown
by the Japanese song or recitative " Sayanara " (in
English, " Farewell ").*　No listener to this can I

* From the *Miyako-Dori*, edited by Mr. Paul Bevan.

think deny that it is simply an idealization of the vocal utterances which strong feeling of a relevant kind might naturally produce. And then if, after this, he listens to Schubert's " Adieu " he may recognize a further idealization of the appropriate musical phrases and cadences—a further development of the melodic form.

Supposing that the above explanations and the above further evidences do not convince dissentients, there may be put to them the question—How then do you explain the origin of music? Were belief in the supernatural as dominant now as during past generations, there would come the ready answer that men when created were endowed with a musical sense; to which, however, would come the reply that some races of men have no musical sense. But now that supernaturalism has been so largely deposed by naturalism, and now that the evolution even of human faculties is by many admitted, there presents itself the question—From what has the musical faculty been evolved? With the established doctrine that from simple vocal signs of ideas language has been developed, there must obviously go the doctrine that from similarly rude beginnings there has been a development of music; and if so there must be faced the question—What rude beginnings? Those who reject the answer here given are bound to give another. What can it be?

DEVELOPED MUSIC.

To dissipate utterly the supposition that the essay " On the Origin and Function of Music " was intended to be a theory of music at large, it may be well to indicate the scope of such a theory: showing, by implication, how small a part of it is included in the essay named. But let me first re-state some of the leading propositions of that essay, and give some additional evidences.

With the truth that music under all its forms is an expression of exalted feeling, must be joined the truth that the exalted feeling which most commonly manifests itself vocally, is one of joy. We see this among children especially. Hence through association it happens that there is a certain vague elation derived from the mere perception of music, even when distance renders its special nature indistinguishable: a faint wave of pleasure arises from sympathy with the half-audible sounds expressive of excited emotion. And this undefined gratification which music at large produces, seems always to remain the background on which each piece of music imposes its

61

particular shape—the faint general feeling which each piece specializes and intensifies, now in this way, now in that.

An associated universal fact must be named, because, though conspicuous, its significance is not sufficiently appreciated. It is that the various musical expressions of feeling in songs and instrumental pieces have all the trait of rhythmical variation—ascents and descents—originally simple and becoming gradually complex. How much closer than we commonly suppose is the resulting kinship among musical compositions, will be seen on comparing the following four diagrams, by which a graphic form is given to the successive ascents and descents and the lengths of successive notes. Of course the intervals between notes and the lengths of notes, are incommensurable quantities; and as, for convenience, the horizontal lines representing the lengths of notes have been made short in comparison with the vertical lines representing the lengths of intervals, a somewhat distorted impression is given. But this leaves unaffected the general likeness which runs throughout these symbolized songs, widely different as they are in their characters. For they represent respectively the " Marseillaise," Handel's " Largo," " Pur di cesti," and a hunting song, " Old Towler."

THE MARSEILLAISE

HANDEL'S LARGO

PUR DI CESTI

OLD TOWLER

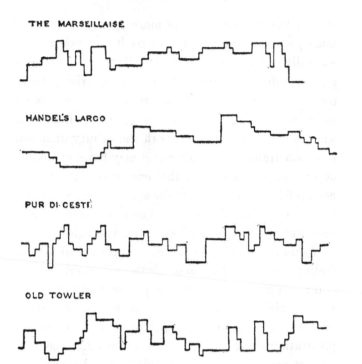

Vocal sounds are produced by the strains of certain muscles, and we see how in each case these strains alternate between extremes, and how the major alternations are broken by minor alternations. Moreover there is suggested the analogy between these alternating muscular strains and those by which dancing is produced: the two having a common origin in the discharge of feeling into action.

On turning now to the more special aspects of music, we have first to note that it has two fundamentally distinct elements—sensational and relational. Its effects are divisible into those arising from tones themselves and those arising from combinations among tones, successive and simultaneous. There needs no proof that both the beauty of music and such dramatic character as it may have, primarily depend on the natures of the tones used—their loudness, pitch, and *timbre*. Quite apart from any organization of them, the sounds taken individually are causes of emotion, now pleasurable, now painful.

Loud tones being ordinarily expressive of strong feelings, it results that in music there is a certain general relation between loudness and intensity of effect. I say advisedly a general relation, because emotions of some kinds, and other emotions at some stages, by prostrating the heart and thus diminishing the outflow of energy, produce muscular relaxation instead of muscular strain; and consequently express themselves in feeble tones. But while recognizing this qualifying truth, which is duly recognized in the appropriate forms of musical expression, we may still say that volume of sound is a sign of mass of feeling, and is in music thus interpreted both by performer and auditor. Here, however, comes in a further truth scarcely at all recognized by either. The loud tone expressive of strong feeling is not forced but spontaneous—is due not to a voluntary but to an involuntary excitement of the vocal apparatus. Consequently a singer's loud tone must be a tone not suggestive of effort: the muscular strain required must be actually or apparently unconscious. But singers, professional and amateur, rarely fulfil this requirement; since, usually, their voices are not sonorous enough. It results that the musical effect is vitiated in a double way: the tone is not of the right quality, and the listener's disagreeable sympathy with the singer's exertion, deducts from the pleasurable consciousness, even if it does not produce a displeasurable consciousness. Hence the unsatisfactoriness of nearly all singing. Indirectly, a contrast of allied origin arises between that kind of instrumental music in which effort manifestly accompanies the production of tones, and that in which the production of tones has no manifest concomitant of effort. In this respect orchestral effects do not compare well with the effects of a grand organ. In the one case the separate tones mostly lack that volume which is a large element in musical satisfaction; while there is an unavoidable consciousness of the exertions which the many performers are making, and sympathy with these, as well as attention to the visible motions, deduct from the pleasure produced. In the other case, by their greater volume the tones excite more fully the emotions appealed to, while the efforts of the organist, usually invisible, neither distract the attention nor excite any sympathetic strain.

I pass now to the question of pitch. In the original essay referred to above, I said much about the relations of high, medium, and low tones to feelings of different kinds, and about their consequent uses in music. A fact not there named must here be emphasized. Alike in passionate speech and in music, the loudest tones are also the tones which diverge most widely from the middle notes of the scale. This is a necessary implication. The two traits go together because both imply great muscular strain. Hence results the ordinary law of expression. The fact is familiar that in musical phrases, single and successive, increasing ascent is accompanied by increasing loudness, and succeeding cadences ending in notes of medium pitch by decreasing loudness: the converse relations in passages below the middle notes being also observable when they occasionally occur. How essential is this relation (allowing for exceptions due to a cause above indicated) will be seen on observing the absurd effect produced if a passage be so played on the piano as to invert these contrasts. And here this reference to the piano suggests a further indirect evidence that music is evolved as alleged; for otherwise no reason can be given why in instrumental music this same law of expression is followed —no reason why high notes should be louder than medium notes. Vocal music is governed by the physiological need, and instrumental music is obliged to follow its lead; thus showing that it has the same genealogy.

Concerning the quality or *timbre* of tones, it must suffice to say that because they indicate certain feelings, certain kinds of tones are appropriate to certain musical settings of words and inappropriate to others. A ridiculous effect would be produced by playing Mozart's " Addio " on the bagpipes; but if the bagpipes be used for rendering " Scots wha' hae," no such extreme incongruity is manifest: the rasping character of the tones is not at variance with the passion expressed. Conversely, if the " Marseillaise " be played on the flute, anyone may perceive that the tones lack adequate power, and do not imply strenuousness. To express the sentiment the tones of the trumpet are the fittest. As under strong emotions of the unsympathetic class the voice acquires a metallic ring, seemingly caused by increase of the overtones, instruments which produce overtones in large proportion are the best for expressing them; while, for the gentler emotions, instruments which yield almost pure tones are better. Of course these truths are empirically recognized. I name them only to fill up the outline of my argument.

Incidentally a good deal has been said above concerning the relational element in music, for it has been impossible to treat of tones simply as tones without reference to other tones. We have now to deal with the relational element exclusively. Let us contemplate the facts from the evolution point of view. In its correspondence with the general theory of evolution we shall find support for the special theory of musical evolution which here concerns us.

In those examples with which Sir Hubert Parry commences his chapter on " Folk-Music," we have vocal utterances little above the howls and groans in which inarticulate feeling expresses itself. There is but an imperfect differentiation of the tones into notes properly so called. So that we see well exemplified that indefiniteness which characterizes incipient evolution in general; and already we have seen that indefiniteness continues to characterize the partially-differentiated tones of savage chants and songs.

Another trait of incipient evolution meets us in the monotonous repetition of rude musical phrases in primitive music, choral and individual. A practice common among the lower races (by no means unknown among the higher) is that when a number combine in an action of a continuous kind, they accompany it by a chant: instance the palanquin-bearers of India; instance various peoples when they join in rowing. Some simple words suggested by the occasion, and droned out in a simple cadence, are repeated in unison by all. And then, sometimes, a change is made to other words with another musical phrase similarly reiterated. Among tribes in the earliest stages the like happens with solos. A few words uttered in tones expressive of joy or grief recur over and over again; showing a natural tendency which even among ourselves may often be witnessed under sudden disaster: " Oh dear me," " Oh dear me," " Oh dear me," being uttered time after time in the same tones. An example yielded by the aborigines of Australia is given by Sir Hubert Parry on page 49 of his *Art of Music*. The significant fact is that one of these monotonous chants or songs, displays the incoherence of a product which is but little evolved; since it may be broken at any point indifferently. Its component passages are not tied together by anything constituting them a whole. Then, once more, one of these primitive pieces of music, if it can be so called, is relatively homogeneous: it is a string of parts all alike. Thus we have the relatively indefinite, incoherent, homogeneity with which evolution begins.

But this is not the only kind of primitive music. There has to be added that kind generated by the emotion with which great achievements are narrated. We read that existing peoples, the Araucanians, sing the prowess of their heroes, and that the Greenlanders sing of " their exploits in the chase " and " chant the deeds of their ancestors " (*Essays*, vol. ii, pp. 433–4): thus reminding us of the early Greek poets.

Now a narrative does not allow repetitions of words, and, by implication, does not allow those repetitions of musical phrases in which repeated words are uttered. A concomitant is that there is no tendency towards rhythm. Though there by-and-by arises a metrical form, yet the rhythm of feet in the verses is too rapid to lend itself to the rhythm of musical phrases. And now, recognizing that this original narrative-music, allied to recitative, does not tend towards repeated phrases and consequent rhythm, yet we may infer that it possibly gives origin to a higher type of music by the importation of these. A simile used in the preceding pages implied that a new character may be given to a simple fabric by superposing a pattern, though the two are alike in material, and though the result is achieved merely by complication of the same apparatus. Here the suggestion arises that possibly there began an occasional superposing on the recitative, of the repeated phrases and the accompanying rhythm above described, and that so a species of melody was produced. Or, conversely, it may have been that passages of recitative came to be intercalated in the choral or solo forms of the repeated phrases. In either way it seems not improbable that there was a mutual influence conducive to the development of melody proper.

Be this as it may, however, traces of development can be recognized. The first step is early indicated.

After repetition of the same simple phrase for a length of time, there is often a transition to another simple phrase which is similarly repeated, and then, by-and-by, a return to the first. We are thus shown the germs of those compoundings characterizing developed music. Repetition of a phrase or of a clause is perhaps the commonest trait in melodies. Taken by itself this yields that intellectual pleasure which we have in the recognition of likeness—a pleasure which, though lost in satiety if the phrase perpetually recurs, is an appreciable pleasure when it recurs once or twice only. Then the second germ which these primitive songs or chants contain, we see in the transition to a different phrase, which is similarly reiterated to weariness, but which, in developed music, is dwelt on only to the extent needed for yielding the pleasure of contrast. Here is the beginning of those multitudinous effects gained by changes of theme, now simple now elaborate, which composers utilize. A further advance occurs when the same phrase is repeated in a higher or lower part of the stave. This is the simplest form of a trait which, as a means to enhanced pleasure, is a trait of Art in general—the union of likeness with difference. For if we recognize the activity of the perceptive faculties at large as being pleasurable, it results that along with the pleasure which perception of similarity gives, there goes the pleasure arising from concomitant perception of dissimilarity: the volume of agreeable consciousness is increased. Then, in pursuance of the same principle, there comes that combination of likeness with difference which is achieved by minor variations of each theme—divergences yielding pleasure from the simultaneous recognition of the agreement and the disagreement.

To trace the growing complications as music develops would need the knowledge of a composer, and would too much encumber the argument. It must suffice here to note that the gratification due to perception of similarity is gradually extended to larger combinations of phrases and clauses and sentences; that the pleasure caused by contrast between one complex of notes and another comes to embrace longer and more elaborate complexes; that recognitions of variety in unity are also achieved on greater scales; that there arise the likenesses and differences due to variations of strength, variations of time, changes of key, &c.; and that, simultaneously, there arises the immense collateral development of harmony: the result being an ever-growing heterogeneity.

Next we have to note a gradual increase of definiteness. This is shown in several ways. There are the requirements that each note shall occur exactly in its place; that it shall have the right pitch; that the intervals shall be correct; and that the lengths

of bars and notes shall be carefully observed: proof
being yielded by the shock that a wrong note
gives and the annoyance arising from a defect in
time.

Then, again, the increasing integration is variously displayed. While the whole piece is held together by subordination to its key-note, it is held
together by the relations between similar phrases as
well as between them and contrasted phrases, severally raising expectations which must be fulfilled; and
it is held together by the relations of its larger parts
—as when after a theme duly elaborated there is
change to another theme markedly different though
congruous, and then presently a return to the original theme: a sense of incompleteness arising if these
divisions are not all there. Thus there is a simultaneous advance in heterogeneity, in integration, and
in definiteness.

But now after noting the traits of evolving music
which exemplify the traits of evolution at large, let
us, so far as we may, observe how there arise different
kinds of music, some of them bearing but indistinct
traces of their origin. We saw that the musical utterances prompted by feeling are mostly expressive
of simple elation—an overflow of good spirits such as
is shown by children dancing around and chanting
some nursery rhyme, as well as by artisans whistling
or humming while at work; and it was suggested that

6

from this association of pleasurable feeling with vocal manifestations of it, arises the vague pleasure caused by musical sounds even when indistinctly audible. This connexion between spontaneous vocalization and agreeable mood of mind, is unspecific in the sense that it does not result in particular musical phrases. The raised feeling prompts vocal movements of any and every kind, just as, when very strong, it prompts irregular dancing about.

But though vocal utterances of raised feeling assume nearly all forms, there are classes of feelings expressed only by vocal utterances more or less specialized: instance those of melancholy, pity, tenderness, as well as others of anger, courage, defiance, &c.: a truth which becomes obvious if sympathetic words are uttered in tones like those used in indignation. But phrases and cadences of these classes vary much. Many persons are almost incapable of expressing by ascents and descents of voice any of the gentler feelings, while there are others whose modulations clearly imply their presence; and it is evident that combinations of tones like theirs may be developed into others which are still more expressive. If, with this idea in mind, Beethoven's *Adelaide*, or some of Gluck's melodies, be contemplated, many of the cadences may be recognized as idealized forms of the appropriate emotional utterances. And if Mendelssohn's " Songs without Words " be listened to, it may be perceived that some of the musical phrases suggest sentiments that are vaguely conceivable.

Here, then, are implied two types of music, the first of which, expressing pleasure in general, is not bound to certain classes of figures, and hence admits of unlimited expansion and variation; and the second of which, expressing feelings more or less special, must use figures that are restricted in their range. It is the non-recognition of this broad distinction which has caused most of the opposition my views have met with.

To explain why certain groups of notes are fitted or unfitted for one or other purpose, seems impossible. But limiting our attention to the great mass of music—the music of exhilaration—we may recognize a contrast between the music of coarse exhilaration and the music of refined exhilaration. In a postscript to the original essay, I named the fact that if, after creasing a piece of paper and then opening it out, an irregular figure be made with ink on one of the folds and the other pressed down upon it, producing a blotted repetition, a certain decorative effect is obtained from the symmetry, ugly as the original line may be; and I suggested that, in like manner, symmetrical arrangements of ugly musical phrases yield an effect attractive to the uncultured: musical doggerel, we may call it, exemplified in music-hall songs and in most of the performances which please those (well-dressed and ill-dressed) who stand round bands at the sea-side. Turning from the music of coarse exhilaration we note that whatever be the cause—probably a physiological one—certain successions of notes and phrases are intrinsically agreeable, irrespective of effects produced by their combinations. Out of these are woven the musical pieces we may distinguish as those of refined exhilaration; since, apart from the beauties of symmetry, and contrast, and structure at large, their component phrases taken singly yield some pleasure, though they do not excite distinct emotions. As instances may be named many of Cherubini's overtures and many of Mozart's sonatas: compositions in which there is little beyond a more or less skilful putting together of musical figures that are individually without much interest.

Finally we come to music of the highest type— poetical music. Of course this is not sharply marked off from the last any more than the last is from its predecessor; for in the music of refined exhilaration there may be used phrases and figures which, though not distinctly emotional, suggest such sentiments as are produced, say, by beautiful surroundings or the prospect of quiet pleasures. Beethoven's " Pastoral Symphony " may be named in illustration. But in the highest type of music the phrases, cadences, and larger figures, are appropriate to stronger emotions of the kinds enumerated above. And here beyond the pleasure yielded by an elaborated pattern having forms pleasing by their likenesses and unlikenesses, we have the sympathetic pleasure yielded by these idealized utterances which we can imagine expressing our own emotions, had we the requisite musical genius. In addition to the beauty of the composition, there is the beauty of the components. Of illustrations, that which comes first to mind is Beethoven's Septet; and I may join with this a piece of another class which is undeservedly neglected — Haydn's " Seven Last Words."

To end these hints towards an exposition of a vast subject let me now bring in an analogy. Already I have said or implied that those who combat the hypothesis here defended, not looking at things from the evolution point of view, do not bear in mind that in course of time there arise complicated products out of simple germs. See, for instance, what has happened with the clothing of birds. Feathers were originally protective. Saying nothing of those forming the wings, which fulfil another purpose, it is clear that those covering the body originally had for their use, and still have in chief measure, the preservation of heat. Here appearance was of little importance. Passing over cases in which colours that aid concealment are acquired, we see that very generally colours subserve the end of increasing sexual attractiveness: an end superposed on, and quite unlike, the original

end. And occasionally there result feathers utterly
unfit for the original end. The gigantic ones forming
a peacock's tail, with their brilliant eye-spots, might
be supposed never to have had anything to do with
maintaining warmth; and there are others, as those
in the crest of a Bird of Paradise, which have almost
lost the traces of a structure appropriate for covering.
Yet, undeniably, they are all modifications of protective appendages. Their secondary characters have
disguised and almost obliterated their primary ones.
In like manner, then, it has happened that out of
phrases and cadences of emotional utterance—some
expressing exhilaration and others expressing more
special feelings—there have been evolved in the
course of ages musical combinations, some characterized by idealized forms of such phrases and others
showing no apparent relation to such phrases; but all
of them woven into gorgeous compositions differing
from their rudiments as much as the plumage of a
kingfisher differs from that of a sparrow.

ESTIMATES OF MEN.

SPEAKING broadly, we may say that the world is always wrong, more or less, in its judgments of men —errs by excess or defect. Judgments are determined less by intellectual processes than by feelings; and feelings are swayed this way or that way largely by mere personal likes and dislikes, or by the desire to express authorized opinions—to be in the fashion. Hence a way of discounting opinions is desirable. Some guidance may be had by observing their oscillations, and noting the stages in their oscillations which at the time being they have reached.

Let me re-state this thesis by setting out with the truth that all movement is rhythmical—that of opinion included. After going to one extreme a reaction in course of time carries it to the other extreme, and then comes eventually a re-reaction. This is clearly observable in the case of reputations. Time was when the authority of Aristotle was supreme and unquestioned. Then came Bacon and the reform in philosophy which he initiated: the result being that the reputation of Aristotle waned and the reputation of Bacon became great. In recent days the over-esti-

mation of Bacon has been followed by a recoil, ending in an under-estimation: one cause being that men
have compared his ideas with those of our time instead of with those of his own time. Meanwhile the
repute of Aristotle has been rising again and now
seems likely to become undue. This rhythm is conspicuously illustrated in the case of Shakespeare, who,
highly appreciated by contemporaries (as witness
Ben Jonson's lines), fell afterwards into neglect, and
then, during the present century, has been continually
rising, until now his position is so high that criticism
is practically paralyzed and societies occupy themselves with the minutiæ of his sentences.

I name these familiar cases merely as illustrating
the suggestion that we may usually form some idea
of the position in which we stand in presence of this
rhythmical movement: recognizing that neither extreme of the judgment on a man is true, and then,
looking at the aggregate evidence, judging whereabouts in the oscillation we are at the time being.
Inspection of the rhythm may lead us to suspect that
the reputation of Shakespeare is at present too high.
The judgment of his devoted admirer Ben Jonson,
who, when told that Shakespeare never blotted out a
line, remarked that he would have done better to blot
a thousand, is probably nearer the mark than the
judgment now current, which implies the belief that
everything he wrote is good. For to any one un-

swayed by fashion, it is manifest that amid the great
mass of that which is supremely excellent, there are
many things far from excellent. Much the same may
be said of Beethoven.

An illustration from our own days will give
greater definiteness to the argument. Early in the
seventies the reputation of George Eliot reached its
zenith. Soon afterwards it began to decline and some
few years ago had fallen to its nadir. Recently a reaction set in. Inspection of these movements will
make it clear that if the estimate of thirty years ago
was in excess, that of five years ago was in defect;
and that hereafter her rank will be considerably
higher than now.

Apart from particular instances, however, the
conclusion is that we ought constantly to find what
are the needful modifications of current opinions—
not opinions about men only but opinions about other
things—by contemplating in each case the rhythm,
and trying to see whereabouts in it we are: feeling
sure that the opinion which prevails is never quite
right, and that only after numerous actions and reac-
tions may it settle into the rational mean.

STATE-EDUCATION.

EARLY in life it became a usual experience with me to stand in a minority—often a small minority, approaching sometimes to a minority of one. At a time when State-education was discussed more as a matter of speculative interest than as a matter of so-called practical politics, I found myself opposed to nearly everyone in expressing disapproval—a disapproval which has continued until now, though with most it has become a political axiom that a government is responsible for the mental culture of citizens.

In the forties this question of education by governmental agency was frequently argued between myself and a valued friend, who in those days wrote letters urging that Church-property should be laid under contribution to provide means. Holding the views I did even at that time respecting the limitation of State-functions,* I opposed, for both general and special reasons. The general reason, allied to reasons which took definite shapes at a later time, was that society is a product of development and not of manu-

---

* Set forth in certain letters on "The Proper Sphere of Government," originally published in 1842 and republished in 1843.

facture. The special reason, harmonizing with this general reason, was that the law of supply and demand extends from the material sphere to the mental sphere, and that as interference with the supply and demand of commodities is mischievous, so is interference with the supply and demand of cultured faculty. Many years later my friend confessed that his experience as a magistrate in Gloucestershire had changed his opinion. It had shown him that education artificially pressed forward, raising in the labouring and artisan classes ambitions to enter upon higher careers, led, through frequent disappointments, to bad courses and sometimes to crime. The general belief he had reached was that mischief results when intellectualization goes in advance of moralization—a belief which, expressed by him in other and less definite words, at first startled me, though it soon became clear that it was congruous with the views I had often urged.

Here I am not about to enter at length on the general question of State-education; otherwise I should demur to the assumption that any government is competent to say what education should be, either in matter, manner, or order; I should contest its right to impose its system of culture upon the citizen, so that under penalty for disobedience his children may be moulded after its approved pattern; and I should deny the equity of taking, through the rates, the earnings of A to pay for teaching the children of B. I should, in short, protest once more against that political superstition which has replaced the divine right of kings by the divine right of parliaments. But I must limit myself to the issue implied above—denying the commonly supposed connexion between intellectual culture and moral improvement; and giving evidence that a society is not benefited but injured by artificially increasing intelligence without regard to character.

To measure the influence for good or evil which a forced intellectual culture produces on a nation, there is no better way than to contemplate the teachings of the daily Press, and to observe the effects wrought. An extremely apt introduction to the subject has recently been exhumed from the pages of *The Idler*. On November 11, 1758, Dr. Johnson wrote as follows:—

" In a time of war the nation is always of one mind, eager to hear something good of themselves and ill of the enemy. At this time the task of news writers is easy. They have nothing to do but to tell that a battle is expected, and afterwards that a battle has been fought, in which we and our friends, whether conquering or conquered, did all, and our enemies did nothing. . . . Among the calamities of war may be justly numbered the diminution of the love of truth by the falsehoods which interest dictates and credulity encourages. A peace will equally leave the warrior and relater of wars destitute of employment, and I know not whether more is to be dreaded from streets filled with soldiers accustomed to plunder, or from garrets filled with scribblers accustomed to lie."

A century and a half seems to have made but little difference. Day by day the reports of the South African war have been full of fictions, exaggerations, garblings: much has been falsified, much suppressed. Instance the statement made soon after the war began, in October, 1899, that the crops of the Boers were rotting on the ground (doubtless originated in London by one who forgot that our autumn corresponds to their spring), and which was followed some months later by the statement that reaping was going on; instance the fact that when the force advancing to relieve Ladysmith was repulsed, the inhabitants were described as receiving the news with equanimity (!), while in due time there came a letter from *The Times* correspondent in Ladysmith describing the " consternation " displayed; instance the reports from the several beleaguered places that the bombardments did no mischief worth mentioning, and then the statement made by Mr. Rhodes after Kimberley was relieved that about 120 were killed or wounded during the siege. Further we have the confession on the part of a special correspondent that misrepresentation was an established policy.

" A false notion of loyalty and patriotism exists in connection with this campaign. Men are branded with the taint of disloyalty if they express the opinion that matters are assuming a critical aspect—unless they describe a defeat as a victory."— *The Globe*, Feb. 26, 1900.

And then another correspondent, Mr. F. Young, himself personally concerned, testified that the military censorship not only suppressed facts but diffused fictions. One more instance. Of the Boers concerning whom, until recently exasperated by farm-burning and women-driving, the accounts given by captured officers and men were uniformly good, and of whom the late Sir George Grey said—" I know no people richer in public and in private virtues than the Boers "—of these same Boers Mr. Ralph, correspondent of the *Daily Mail*, wrote that " they are neither brave nor honourable "; they are " cowardly and dastardly " ; " semi-savage " ; " inhuman " ; filled with " Satanic premeditation," &c.

And thus reports went on during the winter, the spring, the summer: some newspaper readers being made increasingly sceptical by these manifest untruths, while the great mass greedily swallowed, as in Johnson's day, reports good of ourselves and ill of the enemy; until at length from another quarter arrived an example of Press-mendacity striking enough to shake the general faith. There came first the sensational account of a massacre at Pekin, describing in detail the stubborn resistance of the Europeans, the desperate hand-to-hand encounters, the final overwhelming of the small band, followed by particulars of Chinese atrocities; and then there came in a few days proof that this circumstantial account was utterly baseless—there had been no massacre, no

atrocities. Coming home to the public in a more
startling way than had the multitudinous contradic-
tions concerning events in South Africa, this drew
attention to the habitual falsification of news. Proofs
were recalled that telegrams were largely manufactured in Fleet Street: four words being sometimes ex-
panded to 40; so that, as writes "An Old Journalist" in *The Times* of August 29, 1900, " brilliant de-
scriptions of battle scenes filling a column were
evolved from 20 or 30 words of telegraphy." And
the explanation of the system was that the public
appetite for sensational news is so keen that journals
are compelled, as they think, in pursuit of their busi-
ness-interests, to vie with one another in fictitious
and exaggerated reports.

To the foregoing, written in 1900, let me now add
evidence coming in December, 1901, from two eye-
witnesses—the writer of *Unofficial Despatches*, Mr.
Edgar Wallace, and the writer of *With Rimington*,
Capt. L. M. Phillipps. Though these two take opposite views respecting the conduct of the war—the
journalist advocating greater severity, and the captain greater lenity—they are at one in reprobating
the systematic perversion of truth resulting from the
censorship. Mr. Wallace, giving to the Chief Censor
of Lord Roberts' army the title " Lord High Mutila-
tor of Telegraphic Despatches," states that while the
censor would not object to an " unusually optimistic "

despatch, he would, under fear of the commander-in-chief, not dare to pass a pessimistic one, however true it might be (p. 325). Meanwhile Captain Phillipps tells us that the financial gang " had the press in their hands, worked the wires, and controlled and arranged what sort of information should reach England . . . ' grievances ' such as would arrest England's attention . . . were *deliberately invented* " (p. 106) . . . the Boer mortality, sickness, devastation " is a torture long and slow; the agony and bloody sweat. . . . It is most important that the situation should be realized at home, for if it were the conduct of the war would be changed " (p. 211). Thus we have indisputable proof that the nation has been habitually deluded by garbled reports.

And now observe the implications, to introduce which I have set forth these details. London daily journals having circulations amounting altogether to probably three millions, and provincial journals having circulations amounting to at least another three millions, have been daily distributing these falsified reports throughout a population already angered by false statements derived from the Cape Press; thus generating feelings of savage animosity, which were presently exhibited all over the kingdom in brutal treatment of those who ventured to think and to say that the right was not all on our side. And the passions thus manifested were the passions of those who, educated by the State up to the level of newspaper-reading, had been absorbing every day the self-glorifications and the vilifications of the enemy, eagerly looked for. The slumbering instincts of the barbarian have been awakened by a demoralized Press, which would have done comparatively little had not the artificial spread of intellectual culture brought the masses under its influence. Says the Duke in *Measure for Measure*, " There is scarce truth enough alive to keep societies secure "—a saying which, varied to suit the occasion, becomes,—There is scarce truth enough alive to keep societies in health. For the war-fever which has broken out and is working immense mischiefs, not abroad only but in our social state, has resulted from daily breathing an atmosphere of untruth. Is there not reason, then, for the opinion that immense evils may result if intellectualization is pushed in advance of moralization? *

---

* Since this was written there has been furnished to me a marked example of one mode in which public judgments have been habitually perverted: the witness being one whose long experience and high position in the army put him above suspicion of adverse bias—Field-Marshal Sir Neville Chamberlain. He says that "Never before has anything approaching to such wholesale and reckless destruction or abduction of families been enacted by a British Army." At the close of July of this year (1901) he sent to the *Daily Chronicle* a letter in which there were passages akin to the above, blaming our conduct of the South African war. After several days' silence, leading to telegrams of inquiry, he got from the editor a proof with the suggestion that certain adverse passages which contained the pith of the letter should be

7

Other evidence pointing to this conclusion is furnished by the spread of anarchism. Weighed down by the pressure of taxation and aggravated by the demands of militancy, large parts of the populations on the Continent live in a state of chronic discontent. The more cultured among them cannot fail to associate the miseries they bear with a governmental organization which lays hands on their resources and drafts into the army hosts of their younger men; and they are unable or unwilling to recognize the truth that a governmental organization of some kind is necessary, and in a measure beneficent. Besides the constitutionally criminal, those who are led into these erroneous beliefs, and violent acts in pursuance of them, are the educated. Without those facilities for communication which reading and writing and a certain amount of knowledge give them, there could not be formed these schools of anarchy. Here, beyond all doubt, the growth of intellectualization in advance of moralization has done enormous mischief.

We may with certainty say that intellectual culture increases the power which the emotions have of

---

omitted: the result of the delay, and the tacit interdict, being that Sir Neville Chamberlain published the letter in the *Manchester Guardian*. Thus hindrance was put, as it has all along been put, to the publication of opinions at variance with those of the dominant party; while those of the dominant party have been widely diffused. The truth has been suppressed by a censorship at home as well as by a censorship in the field.

manifesting themselves and obtaining their satisfactions — intensifies the emotional life. Were the higher emotions stronger than the lower, this would be an advantage; or were the two balanced it would not be a disadvantage; but, unquestionably, in average human beings the lower emotions are more powerful than the higher: witness the results arising from any sudden removal of all social restraints. Hence, education, adding to the force of all the emotions, increases the relative predominance of the lower, and the restraints which the higher impose are more apt to be broken through. There is a greater liability to social perturbations and disasters.

"So, then, for the sake of social security we are to keep the people in ignorance," will be the exclamation of many on reading the above paragraph. Widely here, as universally on the Continent, the notion is that we must either aid or prevent. There is no recognition of that passive policy which does neither the one nor the other, but leaves things to take their natural course. What has been said above does not imply that the working classes shall be kept in ignorance, but merely that enlightenment shall spread among them after the same manner that it has spread among the upper and middle classes: being privately aided so far as philanthropic feelings prompt; for such feelings and their results are parts of the normal educational agency, operative alike on giver and receiver. But now, while excluding this false interpretation, let me note a strange contrast. Social security is thought so supreme an end that to achieve it citizens may rightly be deprived of their free action and exposed to the risks of death—may upon occasion be seized, made to fight, and perhaps shot while defending the country. This absolute subordination of the individual to the society is in these cases not condemned as unjust or cruel. But in the case before us it is thought cruelly unjust that for the welfare of society the citizen shall be left without public aid in rearing his offspring. Social security being the end common to the two cases, it is in the one thought right that the individual shall be coerced to the extent of risking his life, while in the other it is thought wrong that he shall be left to do his best for himself and children!—wrong not to take other people's property to help him!

One further fact may be emphasized. If supply and demand are allowed free play in the intellectual sphere as in the economic sphere, and no hindrance is put in the way of the naturally superior, education must have an effect widely different from that described—must conduce to social stability as well as to other benefits. For if those of the lower ranks are left to get culture for their children as best they may, just as they are left to get food and clothing for them, it must follow that the children of the superior will be advantaged: the thrifty parents, the energetic, and those with a high sense of responsibility, will buy education for their children to a greater extent than will the improvident and the idle.   And if character is inherited, then the average result must be that the children of the superior will prosper and increase more than the children of the inferior.   There will be a multiplication of the fittest instead of a multiplication of the unfittest.

THE CLOSING HOURS.

In his *Confessions of an English Opium-Eater*, De Quincy says that opium exalted his appreciation of music, and that he commonly took a dose before going to the opera. Accidentally I was once enabled to furnish a testimony of allied kind. Thirty or forty years ago, at times when my nights, always bad, had become unusually bad, I sometimes took a dose of morphia (the effect of which lasts two days) to re-establish, so far as might be, the habit of going to sleep. On one of these occasions it happened that the day after, I went to a concert at which was performed Spohr's Symphony, *The Power of Sound*. Some years before I had heard it with complete indifference, but now I listened to it with considerable pleasure. Partly my sensibility to tones was more acute, and partly there was an increased power of appreciating their relations and the complexes formed of them.

I name these facts as suggesting that between the feelings of early life and those of late life there is a contrast similar to that between the feelings when exalted by a nervous stimulant and the feelings in their ordinary intensity. As by the phlegmatic the

94

elation of the enthusiastic can never be experienced, so in the latter part of life there arises an inability to receive sensations and emotions equally vivid with those of youth and early manhood.

These familiar contrasts imply a contrast which is not so familiar. Commonly regarded as is the truth that as physical strength decreases and the energies decline, the average feelings become weaker (I say the average because exceptions may be pointed out), there is not commonly drawn an obvious corollary respecting the closing stage. Those who think about death, carrying with them their existing ideas and emotions, usually assume that they will have, during their last hours, ideas and emotions of like vividness. It is true that remembered cases in which there occurred incoherence and wandering and inability to recognize persons, show them that when near death the thinking faculty is almost gone; but they do not fully recognize the implication that the feeling faculty, too, is almost gone. They imagine the state to be one in which they can have emotions such as they now have on contemplating the cessation of life. But at the last all the mental powers simultaneously ebb, as do the bodily powers, and with them goes the capacity for emotion in general.

It is, indeed, possible that in its last stages consciousness is occupied by a not displeasurable sense of rest. The feelings accompanying life and all the concomitant desires are no longer conceivable, for to recall them into consciousness implies some mental energy. There remains only such kind of feeling as accompanies entire quiescence—one which, if not absolutely neutral, verges more towards the pleasurable side of consciousness than towards the painful. But however this may be, it is clear that in normal death, or the death of decay, or the death of debility, the sentient state is the farthest possible from that which accompanies vigorous life, or artificially exalted life, and that sensations and emotions all gradually decrease in intensity before they finally cease. Thus the dread of dying which most people feel is unwarranted.

It seems scarcely needful to add that the argument does not apply to the death which follows violence, or that produced by acute disease. In such cases the closing period of indifference is greatly abridged. Up to within a very short time of the end the vital energies remain sufficient to make emotion possible.

STYLE.

FEW openly reject the current belief that a good style implies linguistic culture—implies classical education and study of the best models. The belief seems a rational one, and, often repeated as it is by those in authority, is thought beyond question. Nevertheless it is an invalid belief. Let us first test it by the principles of inductive logic.

Even from the method of agreement, which, if used alone, yields the lowest order of proof, it derives but little support. The great mass of those who have had the discipline which a University gives do not write well. Only here and there in this large class may be found one who is said to have a fine style: for the rest their style is commonplace when not bad. But were the current belief true, a good style should be the rule among the linguistically-cultured—not the exception. Still less justified is the belief when tested by the method of difference. Pursuance of this method should show that writers who have had little discipline in the use of language or none at all do not write well. But again the evidence fails. Everyone knows that from Shakespeare

downwards many good writers have had " little Latin
and less Greek." The untruth of the belief is, however, best shown by critical examination of styles supposed to justify it, or which would justify it were it
true. Already in *The Study of Sociology*, after giving some samples of incoherent English written by
a Prime Minister, a bishop, and a head-master, I
have, in the appendix, subjected to analysis two sentences quoted with approval by Matthew Arnold from
the be-praised Addison: pointing out six faults in
seven lines. Here I propose to continue the criticism
of classically-cultured writers.

The preface to a collection of " golden " verse
ought surely to be a piece of silvern prose—prose
polished and without flaws. And when such a preface
is written by one who achieved classical honours and
has spent his leisure life in the study of literature,
something approaching perfection is to be expected.
It is not found, however. The first sentence of the
preface to Mr. Francis Palgrave's *Golden Treasury*
runs thus:—

"This little Collection differs, it is believed, from others
in the attempt made to include in it all the best original Lyrical
pieces and Songs in our language, by writers not living,—and
none beside the best."

Whether the endeavour to sink the personal in the
impersonal by using the expression " it is believed,"
instead of " I believe," is a trait of good style may

be doubted; since there is given to the reader's mind
a certain needless trouble in substituting the real
meaning for the meaning expressed. Passing over
this, however, let us look at the essential elements
of the sentence. We are told that the collection differs from others. Now a difference between two collections implies inclusion in the one of some thing,
or quality, or trait, not included in the other. Here,
however, the alleged difference consists in " the attempt made to include." But an attempt cannot
form part of a collection. An attempt is neither a
thing, nor a trait, nor a quality, by possession of
which the contents of one collection can be made unlike the contents of another. The *results* of the attempt may make collections differ, but the attempt
itself cannot do so. After passing over six lines we
reach the second paragraph, which opens with these
words:—

"The Editor is acquainted with no strict and exhaustive
definition of Lyrical Poetry; but he has found the task of
practical decision increase in clearness and in facility as he advanced with the work, whilst keeping in view a few simple
principles."

One question suggested by this sentence is—Why say
" the task of *practical* decision "? That the word
practical is superfluous becomes manifest if we ask
what would be the task of *theoretical* decision. Further, this clause is related to the first merely by suggestion, not by specified connexion. What the " prac-

tical decision " is we are not told, but are left to guess.
Again, it is said that " the Editor has found the task
increase in clearness and facility." How can a task
increase in facility? Facility may be gained by one
who undertakes a task and perseveres, but the task
itself remains the same. So that this sentence, like
the other, is incoherent.

The third paragraph begins with these words:—

" This also is all he can plead in regard to a point even
more liable to question;—what degree of merit should give
rank among the Best."

You may question a statement, an opinion, or a belief, for in any one of these something is asserted;
but you cannot question a point, for a point does not
assert anything. That meaning is given by the words
which follow is no adequate defence. Fragments of
sentences are allowable; but then they must be avowedly fragments. A good style does not permit a sentence which by its structure professes to be complete,
but which is meaningless without an appendix.

And then the fourth paragraph opens as follows:—

"It would obviously have been invidious to apply the
standard aimed at in this Collection to the Living."

Now the words " to apply the standard aimed at "
are incongruous. If you *apply* a standard, the implication is that the standard is some species of measure;
but if this is the kind of standard intended, then how

do you aim at it? A thing aimed at must be something at a distance; but if the standard in question is
applied as a measure, it cannot be something distant.
The words do not suggest a consistent idea.

The Academy for January 15, 1898, contains a
notice of " A Forgotten Novel by James Anthony
Froude "; and on page 79 extracts from it are given.
The first begins thus:—

"I take it to be a matter of the most certain experience in
dealing with boys of an amiable infirm disposition, that exactly
the treatment they receive from you they will deserve."
[*Shadows of the Clouds*, p. 22.]

Not dwelling on the opinion expressed, which by the
words " certain " and " exactly " is made far too definite to fit facts of the kinds implied, I go on to say
that the sentence is ill-composed. One of its defects
is verboseness. The first twelve words are equivalent
to " Experience proves." If it be said that the twelve
are more emphatic than the two, I reply that the two
are quite emphatic enough for the occasion. Then
the phrases are anything but classic. The phrase " I
take it to be," though common as a colloquialism, is
scarcely fit for literary use. Why not " I think it
is "? Instead of a direct statement an indirect one
may fitly be adopted if the reader's thought is thus
economized, or if variety of form is needed; but here
an irrelevant idea, " taking," suggested instead of the
relevant idea " thinking," has to be mentally correct-

ed. Nor is the expression " a matter of " to be approved. A word used in many relations calls up indefinite thoughts that have to be shaped by the context; implying a suspension. In the various expressions—" It is a matter of fact," " that's a matter of course," " what's the matter "? " it will cost a matter of £50," we see that the word " matter," divorced from its primary meaning, arouses vague ideas which the mind has to eke out thus or thus according to the adjacent words. Now from a good style are excluded all words having unsettled connotations; save where indefiniteness is intended, which it is not in this case. A more serious objection is that the phrase " I take it to be," is incongruous with the phrase " most certain experience "; for the first does not indicate positiveness whereas the second is absolute. We cannot with propriety link a statement implying some doubt with a statement implying no doubt. It is absurd for a man out in a thunder-shower to say " I take it this is rain," or, " I think it rains "; and it is similarly absurd to join the expression " I think " or its equivalent to a statement of a fact said to be " most certain." Then, again, why " *most* certain "? In careless talk union of the two words is common, but in writing regarded as specially good we ought not to find a word connoting absoluteness preceded by a word connoting degree. Finally, and chiefly, comes the objection that the sentence is of uncertain meaning. To say of the boys indicated " that exactly the treatment they receive from you they will deserve " is to say that if you treat them mildly they will deserve mild treatment, and that if you treat them harshly they will deserve harsh treatment. Surely this cannot be meant! In any case, however, the sentence has the fatal defect that it leaves the reader in doubt.

Another example is furnished by the apostle of culture, Mr. Matthew Arnold. On the page of *The Academy* preceding that from which I have just quoted, there is a laudatory essay on him, under the title "Reputations Reconsidered." In it is reproduced one of his sentences with this introduction:—— " His own judgment was perpetually guided by the principles laid down in a famous passage beginning:——

'There can be no more useful help for discovering what poetry belongs to the class of the truly excellent, and can therefore do us most good, than to have always in one's mind lines and expressions of the great masters, and to apply them as a touchstone to other poetry.'" [*Essays in Criticism*, 2nd ser. p. 16.]

My first remark is that the phrase " useful help " conceals a pleonasm. A help is defined as a thing which aids or assists, and a thing which does that is a useful thing; so that a "useful help" is a useful useful thing. Instead of "no more useful help" he should have written "no better help." We come next to the

clause—" what poetry belongs to the class of the truly
excellent." Why all these words? Whatever belongs to the class of the truly excellent is necessarily
truly excellent. Why then speak of the class? The
phrase should be:—" what poetry is truly excellent."
Then, again, the clause " to apply them as a touchstone " is, to say the least, awkward. Surely it should
be " to apply them as touchstones." Once more, what
is the use of the final words " to other poetry "? The
first part of the sentence has already implied that
" other poetry " is the thing to be tested. Hence,
leaving out intermediate clauses, the statement is that
for discovering what poetry is " truly excellent " certain tests should be applied " to other poetry "! To
convey the intended meaning the sentence should
have run:—There can be no better helps for discovering what poetry is truly excellent, and can therefore
do us most good, than lines and expressions of the
great masters kept always in mind and applied as
touchstones. Or otherwise:—There is no better way
of discovering what poetry is truly excellent, and
can therefore do us most good, than to keep always
in mind lines and expressions of the great masters
and apply them as touchstones. Thirteen words are
saved and the meaning definitely expressed.

In defence it will perhaps be said that these faulty
sentences have been picked out and are exceptional.
This is untrue. As the references imply, they have

not been sought for. The quotations from Mr. Palgrave are respectively the first sentence of his preface
to *The Golden Treasury* and the first sentences of the
next three paragraphs; and beyond reading that preface I have read absolutely nothing of his. The quotation from Mr. Froude is the opening sentence of
certain passages given by his admiring reviewer. And
the sample of Mr. Matthew Arnold's writing which
I have analyzed is the only prose sentence his eulo-
gist reproduces. A fair inference is that sentences
similarly faulty are common in the works of these
three authors.

STYLE *CONTINUED.*

LET it not be supposed that styles free from such defects as I have pointed out, are therefore to be classed as good styles. I am far from saying or implying this. Other traits must be possessed—aptness of words, variety of form, freshness of metaphor, euphony—traits which, as I know to my regret, innate faculty alone can achieve. My position is that a style cannot be redeemed by any or all of these traits if its sentences are incoherent, or contain superfluities and duplications of meaning. Avoidance of defects of construction is a primary requisite; and praise cannot be given to a culture which, promising to insure a good style, does not insure its first element.

It seems strange that the current *a priori* conclusion respecting the effects produced by the study of languages and by familiarity with good models, is not verified *a posteriori.* The absence of verification emphasizes the French saying, "The Style is the Man."

A personal experience has strengthened my belief in this saying. More than half-a-century ago some

106

incident raised in me the inquiry why certain words
and collocations of words are more effective than
others. Up to that time I had paid not the least attention to style. But the problem then presented led
me to consider it from a psychological point of view.
Glances into works on the subject yielded but little
insight: the maxims I met with were purely empirical.
The result was an investigation which ended in the
composition of an essay on " Force of Expression "—
an essay which was refused by the editor of a long-
since deceased periodical, *Fraser's Magazine.* Ten
years later this essay, somewhat improved, was published in *The Westminster Review* under the title
" The Philosophy of Style ": the editor's title, not
mine. One of the conclusions set forth, along with
the reasons supporting it, was that words of Anglo-
Saxon origin (I use the name spite of Mr. Freeman,
since to call them " English " words would here cause
confusion) are more effective than words of Latin
origin. Now this belief, common among others and
strengthened in me on finding it justified by a general principle, ought to have been specially operative
on my style. But recently, when revising *First Principles,* I was struck by the fact that it has not been
at all operative: the language used in that work is
markedly latinized. Of course, dealing largely as the
work does with abstract and general ideas, lack of
Anglo-Saxon words expressing them, necessitated

adoption of words derived from Latin and Greek.
But I found many places where words of home-origin
might have been used instead of words of foreign
origin. It was clear that the current maxim, verified
though it was by my own investigation, had in very
small measure influenced me when writing.

And this comparative absence of influence is explicable enough now that I remember how little I
have been guided by other conclusions set forth in
the essay named—conclusions which I hold still, as
strongly as when they were drawn. They have never
been present to me when writing. From moment to
moment such words and forms of expression as habit
had made natural to me, were used without thought
of their conformity or nonconformity to the principles I had espoused. Occasionally, indeed, when revising a manuscript or a proof, one of these principles
has been recalled and has dictated the substitution of
a word, or the search for a brief phrase to replace a
long one. But the effect has been extremely small.
The general traits of my style have remained unchanged, notwithstanding my wish to change some
of them. There is substantial truth in the French
saying. Varying it somewhat, we may say—style
is organic. Doubtless organization may be modified,
but the function like the structure retains its fundamental characters.

After reading the above paragraphs the reader

will be astonished when I say that I have never studied style. He will think the assertion flatly contradicts much that I have just written. Nevertheless the statement is true in its broad sense. The essay mentioned, on " Force of Expression," which had its origin in a psychological query, of course covered but a small part of the subject. Though when published its title was changed, at the editor's instigation, to " The Philosophy of Style," the substance remained the same; and I was presently blamed by him because it contained as he said " only the backbone of the subject." As was thus implied, the essay ignores those traits of style which give quality, distinction, or colour; and having set forth the psychological conclusions at which I had arrived, I thought nothing about such traits. It never occurred to me either before or since to take any author as a model. Indeed the thought of moulding my style upon the style of any one else is utterly incongruous with my constitutional disregard of authority. Nor have I at any time examined the writing of this or that author with the view of observing its peculiarities. Any criticisms I have passed, any opinions I have formed, have been entirely incidental. Defects such as those above instanced have indeed often drawn my attention—attention which is kept ever awake by criticism of my own writing; but beyond remarking such defects in passing, my observation of style has been limited to recognition of conspicuous traits which I like or dislike. I have been repelled by the ponderous, involved structure of Milton's prose; while, on the other hand, I have always been attracted by the finished naturalness of Thackeray. And from the applause of Ruskin's style I have dissented on the ground that it is too self-conscious—implies too much thought of effect. In literary art, as in the art of the architect, the painter, the musician, signs that the artist is thinking of his own achievement more than of his subject always offend me.

Here, perhaps, I may fitly say of my own style that from the beginning it has been unpremeditated. The thought of style considered as an end in itself, has rarely if ever been present: the sole purpose being to express ideas as clearly as possible and, when the occasion called for it, with as much force as might be. Let me add that some difference has been made by the practice of dictation. Up to 1860 my books and review-articles were written. Since then they have all been dictated. There is a prevailing belief that dictation is apt to cause diffuseness, and I think the belief is well founded. It was once remarked to me by two good judges—the Leweses—that the style of *Social Statics* is better than the style of my later works, and, assuming this opinion to be true, the contrast may I think be ascribed to the deteriorating effect of dictation. A recent experience strengthens me in this conclusion. When finally revising *First Principles*, which was dictated, the cutting out of superfluous words, clauses, sentences, and sometimes paragraphs, had the effect of abridging the work by fifty pages—about one-tenth.

MEYERBEER.

An illustration of that rhythm of opinion commented upon some pages back, is furnished by the reputation of Meyerbeer—once so great, now so small. At one time Liszt maintained that he stood head and shoulders above the rest: " the rest " no doubt meaning composers then living; while Heine wrote—" By this work [*Les Huguenots*] Meyerbeer has won, never again to lose, his citizenship in the eternal city of fine minds, in the Jerusalem of celestial art." At present his name is scarcely heard. *Les Huguenots* is occasionally performed; but among those musically educated I have found none who knew anything of his music, and some who hardly knew his name. There seems no escape from this violent action and reaction, and when men have been raised too high they must pay the penalty of falling too low. But the judicially minded may, in the way already indicated, discount prevailing opinions and form reasonable estimates. When one once so highly lauded comes to be neglected and spoken of contemptuously, we may be sure that the under-estimate errs as did the over-estimate, and from the passing

112

phase of under-estimation may judge approximately where the true place lies. Thus judged, Meyerbeer should unquestionably stand much higher than at present.

He is characterized as " theatrical," with the tacit implication that he produces his effects by display and noise. Was my knowledge of his music derived only from hearing his operas fifty years ago, this charge, made by those whom the prevailing fashion has carried away, might have influenced me; but my opinion is largely based upon familiarity with his music as arranged for the piano, in which the theatrical element is not present. Being thus enabled to judge, I am not afraid to say that the opinion expressed by Liszt was much nearer to the mark than is the current opinion. Among faults alleged against him one is that he is given to arpeggios and scale-passages. Now compositions which, instead of musical thoughts, give us combinations of notes implying no thoughts, always offend me, and hence I was surprised at this assertion. Scale-passages especially annoy me: suggesting that the composer, " gravelled for lack of matter," runs upstairs to find an idea, and being disappointed comes down again. Wishing to see whether arpeggios and scale-passages are really more frequent in Meyerbeer than in others, I requested a lady-pianist who is with me to count the number of them in the first 20 pages of three of his operas, and in three of Mozart's operas.   The results were these:—

Roberto il Diavolo,	25 scale-passages,	20 arpeggios.	
Le Prophète,	18 "	41 "	
Les Huguenots,	15 "	22 "	

making 58 of the one and 83 of the other.   In contrast with these there were in Mozart's—

Don Juan,	60 scale-passages,	31 arpeggios.	
Zauberflöte,	57 "	10 "	
Nozze di Figaro,	58 "	36 "	

making a total of 175 scale-passages and 77 arpeggios.   So that in equal spaces Meyerbeer has 151 of these mechanical successions and Mozart 253.   Thus brought to the test of numbers the charge is effectually disposed of: the " classical " composer Mozart being in a far greater degree open to it.

Then there is the complaint, partly coincident with the last, that his ideas are commonplace.   This, too, surprised me when I met with it, for I am impatient of hackneyed musical ideas.   Sometimes, indeed, to test a composer's originality, I have, while listening, observed whether I could often anticipate, or partially anticipate, the phrases that were coming, or something like them, and when I could, have discounted my estimate of him.   But in this case, as in the preceding one, the comparison with Mozart, instead of proving, disproves the allegation.   When having played to me Mozart's Sonatas I find myself exclaiming " Stop " or " Skip ": the result being that not more than one-third of the movements are marked as worth playing: my feeling respecting the others being that they consist of familiar figures strung together in a new order. When listening to Meyerbeer's operas as arranged for the piano, this impression is not produced. Even in parts which are merely accompaniments to stage-action, though there may be little of interest, there is generally much that is fresh—very few hackneyed phrases.

But my chief reason for ranking Meyerbeer high is that he combines, better than any composer I have heard, the two requisite elements in fine music—dramatic expression and melody. In the scene between Raoul and Valentine in *Les Huguenots*, he succeeds in doing that which Wagner tries to do and, as I think, without success. Notwithstanding all that has been said against him, I shall continue to applaud Meyerbeer until there is shown to me some work in which truth of expression and melodic quality are better united than they are in " Robert, toi que j'aime."

THE PURSUIT OF PRETTINESS.

CRITICISMS on the lives of our neighbours are abundant enough, and some of them turn upon the lack of proportion their lives show—now undue devotion to business, now want of useful occupation, now absorption in a favourite pursuit, and so on. But while the art of living is thus recognized as a subject which concerns everyone, there is no deliberate study of it: haphazard thoughts occupy the place of rational conclusions. None try to estimate the relative values of ends—how much energy may fitly be expended in achieving this class of satisfactions, and how much in achieving that class. Choice is made without any pre-conception of the need for giving each kind of mental or bodily activity its share, and only its share, in the aggregate activity. The result is that all lives are more or less distorted—usually very much distorted.

This general remark is preliminary to a special remark. There is one pursuit which nearly all suppose may be carried on without limit—the pursuit of beauty; or rather, the pursuit of prettiness. Women particularly, by the daily expenditure of their time, imply the belief that the chief business of life is to please the eye. From the American lady whose idea seems to be—Men must work that women may dress, down to the British kitchen-maid, whose pleasure during the week is in the thought of vying with her mistress on Sunday, the ambition which goes before all others is to satisfy the æsthetic want; or rather, to obtain the admiration which is a concomitant, or expected concomitant.

For referring to these familiar facts the excuse here made is that they are parts of much larger facts. Originating as do these feelings concerned with visible beauty in the desire for sex-admiration, and associated as they become with a desire for admiration in general, their influence pervades all actions. A motive which prompts the sacrifices shown us by the cramped feet of the Chinese women and the strangled waists of their European sisters, necessarily forms a dominant element in consciousness at large, and necessarily affects daily life in innumerable ways. Given the implied mental attitude, and the question —" How will it look?" is certain to be a question that perpetually comes to the front. If even bones are bent in the effort to obtain admiration, it is inevitable that there will be a moulding of conduct in all ways with the like aim. Appearance will tend ever to become a primary end and use a secondary end; as with

the savage who struts about in a mantle in fine
weather but takes it off when it rains.

As already said, it is not these immediate results
but the remoter results to which attention needs directing. I do not refer only to such remoter results
as the injuries to health caused by making dress a
thing to look pretty in rather than a thing to be warm
in—dress which, sufficient at one part of the day, at
another part leaves wide surfaces bare; but I refer
to the ways in which this making of appearance an
end supreme over other ends, affects the house at
large and the course of domestic affairs. The cottage-
wife whose small window is so choked with flowers
that little light comes in, is not likely to understand
the consequent evils if they are pointed out; but the
lady to whom you explain that light is an important
factor in the maintenance of health—so important
that patients on the southern side of a hospital re-
cover faster than those on the northern side—and
that therefore the sitting in darkened rooms is detri-
mental, proves no more amenable to reasoning. The
welfare of the carpet is an end she thinks more important than extra health to her family. That the
polished floor, bordering the carpet, often causes mischiefs—bruises, sprains, dislocations—and that even
when no such mischiefs result there is the perpetual
fear which prompts careful stepping, are not reasons
sufficient to counterbalance in her mind the reason

that the polished floor looks well. With the furniture, too, it is the same. The choice has obviously
been determined mainly by the thought of appearance and very little by the thought of comfort. Here
in the bay-window is a seat having its surface cut out
into flowers in high relief; and all around are the
chairs, some of the fashionable type, some archaic in
form, and others having pretty carved patterns, but
nearly all unpleasant to sit in—anti-caller chairs they
might be named.

So with the numerous pretty things, or things supposed to be pretty, which burden the tables, the minor
pieces of furniture, the brackets, and so on, including
such absurdities as paper-knives with fret-work han-
dles. The pleasure derived from them, whether by
owner or guest, is practically nominal: there is little
beyond the consciousness that there are pretty things
all about. Meanwhile, leaving out the question of original cost, they are, in their multitude, constant sources
of vexation. The doings of careless housemaids entail
disturbances of temper which form a large set-off to
any gratifications yielded. Not only, to carry out Bacon's conception, does a man who marries give hostages
to fortune, but also he who accumulates objects of
value; for each affords occasions for Fortune's malice.

And then, after all, this too-eager pursuit of æsthetic satisfactions defeats itself. Beauty is not attained by filling a room with beautiful things. The

total effect of a room so filled is destroyed by the separate effects of its contents. These distract attention from one another, and in their totality distract attention from the room. You may have an artistic interior or you may have a museum, but you cannot have both. It is with the domestic artist as with artists at large—painters, architects, and others—the usual error lies in excess prompted by undue desire for admiration. And here, indeed, we come upon the further fault implied by this absorbing pursuit of æsthetic ends: there is a betrayal of a moral attitude of an inferior kind. Eagerness for applause when made conspicuous, lowers in the minds of others the estimate of one who shows it. And very often it is manifest that this eagerness is the predominant motive. Illustrations meet us everywhere. Over-ornamented rooms are even more numerous than over-dressed women.

But returning from this digressive criticism, I will add only that the way in which the æsthetic end is made to dominate over other ends of more importance, might be illustrated at length from the dining-table; beginning with the choice of a cook not for her culinary skill but for her ability to make pretty dishes; passing on to the acquirement of a taste for imperfectly-cooked vegetables, because sufficient cooking would destroy their bright green (I state facts); and in various ways showing how palatableness and digestibility are sacrificed to a trivial and transitory achievement of good appearance. But enforcement of the thesis has been carried far enough. The general proposition that there is no due proportioning of the various ends of life, has been exemplified in the more special proposition that the æsthetic ends occupy far too large an area of consciousness.

By all means let people have around a few beautiful things on which the eyes may dwell with pleasure day after day; but let not life be distorted by the distracting of attention from essentials. Here are parents whose duty it is to fit children for carrying on life, but who, guided by mere tradition or not even that, have bestowed scarcely a thought on education rationally considered. Here are people required to take part in the direction of social affairs by their votes, who are still guided by the crudest superstitions—" good-for-trade " fallacies and the like—who never dream of fitting themselves for their functions as citizens. And on all sides are those who ignore the natural world around, animate and inanimate, the understanding of which in its essential principles concerns alike the right conduct of life and the conception of human existence. Meanwhile endless care and thought are daily bestowed on a multiplicity of things which are expected to bring admiration; though, whether things worn or things displayed as ornaments, they as often as not do the reverse.

9

PATRIOTISM.

WERE any one to call me dishonest or untruthful he would touch me to the quick. Were he to say that I am unpatriotic, he would leave me unmoved. " What, then, have you no love of country? " That is a question not to be answered in a breath.

The early abolition of serfdom in England, the early growth of relatively-free institutions, and the greater recognition of popular claims after the decay of feudalism had divorced the masses from the soil, were traits of English life which may be looked back upon with pride. When it was decided that any slave who set foot in England became free; when the importation of slaves into the Colonies was stopped; when twenty millions were paid for the emancipation of slaves in the West Indies; and when, however unadvisedly, a fleet was maintained to stop the slave-trade; our countrymen did things worthy to be admired. And when England gave a home to political refugees and took up the causes of small states struggling for freedom, it again exhibited noble traits which excite affection. But there are traits, unhappily of late more frequently displayed, which do the reverse. Contemplation of the acts by which England has acquired over eighty possessions—settlements, colonies, protectorates, &c.—does not arouse feelings of satisfaction. The transitions from missionaries to resident agents, then to officials having armed forces, then to punishments of those who resist their rule, ending in so-called " pacification "—these processes of annexation, now gradual and now sudden, as that of the new Indian province and that of Barotziland, which was declared a British colony with no more regard for the wills of the inhabiting people than for those of the inhabiting beasts—do not excite sympathy with their perpetrators. Love of country is not fostered in me on remembering that when, after our Prime Minister had declared that we were bound in honour to the Khedive to reconquer the Soudan, we, after the re-conquest, forthwith began to administer it in the name of the Queen and the Khedive—practically annexing it; nor when, after promising through the mouths of two Colonial Ministers not to interfere in the internal affairs of the Transvaal, we proceeded to insist on certain electoral arrangements, and made resistance the excuse for a desolating war.* Nor

---

* We continue to hear repeated the transparent excuse that the Boers commenced the war. In the far west of the U.S., where every man carries his life in his hand and the usages of

does the national character shown by a popular ova-
tion to a leader of filibusters, or by the according
of a University honour to an arch-conspirator, or by
the uproarious applause with which undergraduates
greeted one who sneered at the " unctuous rectitude "
of those who opposed his plans of aggression, appear
to me lovable. If because my love of country does
not survive these and many other adverse experiences
I am called unpatriotic—well, I am content to be so
called.

To me the cry—" Our country, right or wrong! "
seems detestable. By association with love of country the sentiment it expresses gains a certain justification. Do but pull off the cloak, however, and the
contained sentiment is seen to be of the lowest. Let
us observe the alternative cases.

Suppose our country is in the right—suppose it
is resisting invasion. Then the idea and feeling embodied in the cry are righteous. It may be effectively
contended that self-defence is not only justified but is
a duty. Now suppose, contrariwise, that our country
is the aggressor—has taken possession of others' territory, or is forcing by arms certain commodities on
a nation which does not want them, or is backing
up some of its agents in " punishing " those who

---

fighting are well understood, it is held that he is the aggressor
who first moves his hand towards his weapon. The application
is obvious.

have retaliated. Suppose it is doing something which, by the hypothesis, is admitted to be wrong. What is then the implication of the cry? The right is on the side of those who oppose us; the wrong is on our side. How in that case is to be expressed the so-called patriotic wish? Evidently the words must stand—"Down with the right, up with the wrong!" Now in other relations this combination of aims implies the acme of wickedness. In the minds of past men there existed, and there still exists in many minds, a belief in a personalized principle of evil—a Being going up and down in the world everywhere fighting against the good and helping the bad to triumph. Can there be more briefly expressed the aim of that Being than in the words—"Up with the wrong and down with the right"? Do the so-called patriots like the endorsement?

Some years ago I gave expression to my own feeling—anti-patriotic feeling, it will doubtless be called—in a somewhat startling way. It was at the time of the second Afghan war, when, in pursuance of what were thought to be "our interests," we were invading Afghanistan. News had come that some of our troops were in danger. At the Athenæum Club a well-known military man—then a captain but now a general—drew my attention to a telegram containing this news, and read it to me in a manner implying the belief that I should share his anxiety. I astounded him by replying—" When men hire themselves out to shoot other men to order, asking nothing about the justice of their cause, I don't care if they are shot themselves."

I foresee the exclamation which will be called forth. Such a principle, it will be said, if accepted, would make an army impossible and a government powerless. It would never do to have each soldier use his judgment about the purpose for which a battle is waged. Military organization would be paralyzed and our country would be a prey to the first invader.

Not so fast, is the reply. For one war an army would remain just as available as now—a war of national defence. In such a war every soldier would be conscious of the justice of his cause. He would not be engaged in dealing death among men about whose doings, good or ill, he knew nothing, but among men who were manifest transgressors against himself and his compatriots. Only aggressive war would be negatived, not defensive war.

Of course it may be said, and said truly, that if there is no aggressive war there can be no defensive war. It is clear, however, that one nation may limit itself to defensive war when other nations do not. So that the principle remains operative.

But those whose cry is—" Our country, right or

wrong!" and who would add to our eighty-odd possessions others to be similarly obtained, will contemplate with disgust such a restriction upon military
action. To them no folly seems greater than that of
practising on Monday the principles they profess on
Sunday.

SOME LIGHT ON USE–INHERITANCE.

THE parable of the mote and the beam has applications in the sphere of science as in other spheres. One striking instance of its aptness is furnished by the controversy between the neo-Darwinians and the neo-Lamarckians—to use, for the nonce, two inappropriate but convenient names. Contending for the sufficiency of natural selection, those of the Weismann school say to their antagonists—Where are your facts? (deliberately ignoring, by the way, sundry facts that are assignable). To these the rejoinder made by the believer in use-inheritance may fitly be —Where are *your* facts? If the one insists upon inductive proof the other may also do this, and there is no inductive proof whatever of natural selection. Of the effects of artificial selection the evidence is overwhelming, but of the effects of natural selection none is forthcoming. Nature cannot select as a breeder does with a view to increasing some one trait, but can select only those individuals which, by the aggregate of their traits, are the best fitted for living. Until the production of one species by natural selec-

128

tion is shown, there is not even the beginning of inductive proof. On the other hand inductive proof of the use-inheritance doctrine is not wholly wanting. Yet, perpetually, the neo-Darwinians say to the neo-Lamarckians—Where are your facts?

The controversy yields a further illustration of the way in which men who see clearly the defects in their opponents' hypotheses cannot see the like defects in their own hypotheses. The doctrine of use-inheritance is rejected because of inability to " conceive any means " by which a modification produced in an organ, can produce a correlated modification in the germ of a descendant. Yet the alternative hypothesis is accepted notwithstanding a kindred inability which is certainly not less and may be held much greater. If Weismann's view is true, such a structure as a peacock's tail-feather implies over 300,000 determinants. Multiply that by the number of such feathers and add those of the body-feathers, as well as those of all the parts of all the organs, and then imagine the number of determinants which must be contained in the microscopic sperm-cell. Further, imagine that in the course of the developmental transformations, each determinant finds its way to the place where it is wanted! Surely to " conceive any means " by which these requirements may be fulfilled, is not a smaller difficulty if it is not a greater.

Thus far I have dealt with preliminaries needful

for understanding that which is now to follow. Nature presents us with certain phenomena showing conclusively that structural processes may be effected by some play of unseen agencies; though the mode in which they can be effected is inconceivable. Two instances near akin will suffice.

The beauty of snow-crystals has filled many with delight, but few have speculated about the strange facts implied by their forms. Though infinitely varied, they are all of hexagonal type in the arrangements of their parts, and they are absolutely symmetrical. If one of the rays bears at a certain spot a projection on one side there is a corresponding equal projection on the other side; and on every ray throughout the aggregate there are identical pairs of appendages. If in one place there is a complex appendage there are like complex appendages at all of the answering places. How is this symmetry achieved? We have no alternative but to suppose that as the snow-crystal descends quietly through the upper air charged with watery vapour, accretion of a molecule of water at one point is instantly followed by accretions at all the corresponding points, and that this is effected by the coercive agency of the entire aggregate. Polar forces are said to constitute the agency; but of these forces we know nothing. The molecular actions by which these beautiful structures are built up are inconceivable.

Contemplate now a more wonderful phenomenon of the same order. Everyone has from time to time observed on a bedroom window after a sharp frost, a film of crystallized water covering the insides of the panes, and everyone has admired the foliaceous forms assumed: few, however, pausing to think how such forms can originate. In *Nature* for February 7, 1901, Prof. T. G. Bonney gives a striking account of such structures produced not on a window but on a pavement.

"They form divergent groups, like the sticks of a partly opened fan . . . groups, often half a yard in diameter, composed of frond-like radiating tufts, made up of thin stems or acicular crystals (often some four inches long and about the thickness of a bodkin) beautifully curved: this almost invariable bending of the 'blades' being the most marked characteristic. They resemble very delicate seaweeds, dried and displayed on a card as an ornamental group."

On considering the actions producing these arrangements, we are obliged to conclude that the crystallization goes on in each part under the control of all other parts. If the union of water-molecules into crystals took place at every point independently, or under local influences only, there could not be that subordination of the details to the whole which produces the symmetrical frond-like structure. We must assume that while forming, the entire aggregate of crystals coerces the molecules in each place, while these in their turn join the rest in coercing those in every other place. On the one

hand it is impossible to deny this orderly subordination of parts to the whole, and the reactive influence on the whole exercised by each part; and
yet, on the other hand, we cannot " conceive any
means " by which these marvellous structural processes are effected. The thing is done but it is impossible to imagine how it is done.

The bearing of these cases upon the doctrine of
use-inheritance is obvious. We are shown that impossible though it may be to conceive how any structural modification in one part of an organism can
affect the sperm-cells or germ-cells in such way as to
give their product a proclivity towards a corresponding structure, yet it is not unreasonable to suppose
that they are thus affected. That the play of forces
by which such a relation is established is unimaginable, is, as we here see, no reason for asserting that
there does not exist such a play of forces.

And, indeed, when we call to mind those advances
in molecular physics and the physics of the ether
which have immensely exalted our ideas of the processes everywhere going on, we may perceive that
the hypothesis of use-inheritance is not at all incongruous with known facts. Now that by electric waves
signals are made without wires a thousand miles
away; now that Röntgen rays are shown to penetrate
various substances opaque to light; now that from
uranium and other bodies are found to emanate spe-

cial classes of rays which are able temporarily to endow other kinds of matter with like powers of radioactivity; now when we are shown that besides that agitation of molecules constituting heat, the molecules of solid substances give and receive other orders of oscillations; we may suspect that the molecular influences permeating living bodies transcend our conceptions. It is probable that each group of specially-arranged molecules composing the constitutional unit of an organism, is a centre from which there radiate the undulations produced by each of its multitudinous components; and that such undulations, diffused throughout the organism, affect the corresponding components of other such units: tending to produce like oscillations and congruous structures. We may infer that there ever goes on a process like that above implied, under which the entire aggregate coerces into harmonious forms all the minute molecular aggregates composing it, while each of these has its share in modifying the rest; and that thus any local change of structure becomes a cause of change in all the constitutional units, and, among others, those contained in sperm-cells and germ-cells. Moreover if, as elsewhere suggested (*Biology*, §§ 54*d*, 97*f*), there is a circulation of protoplasm, this universal assimilation of characters must be greatly facilitated. Be this as it may, however, the remarkable phenomena above described make it clear that in-

ability to " conceive any means " by which acquired
characters impress themselves on the reproductive
elements, is no adequate reason for assuming that
they cannot do this.

Let me add that much more simply, and still more
conclusively, may this objection raised by the neo-
Darwinists to the hypothesis of use-inheritance, be
disposed of. Huyghens rejected the theory of gravitation. What was his reason? He said that such an
attraction as was implied could not be explained by
any principles of mechanics. That is to say, he could
not " conceive any means " by which the mutual influence of the attracting bodies could be effected.
Nevertheless the theory of gravitation was established by irrefragable proofs, and has long been universally accepted.

Of course the foregoing paragraphs should form
a part of *The Principles of Biology*. But as, in 1899,
I issued a finally-revised edition of that work, and
see no probability that I shall ever be able to issue
another, I decide to include them here.

PARTY-GOVERNMENT.

THERE is a truth, familiar to every one, over which I often marvel—that tremendous results frequently follow small and apparently irrelevant causes. In *The Study of Sociology*, Chapter XIII, I have pointed out that the organic and super-organic sciences illustrate in an eminent degree what I there called " fructifying causation." In the phenomena they deal with, the " multiplication of effects," seen in Evolution at large, is transcendent in degree. A disease-germ, getting into the body, produces complex derangements great and small throughout numerous organs; and, if recovery takes place, *sequelæ* are often such as affect disastrously the remainder of life. Similarly in a society, such a simple occurrence as the discovery of gold brings multitudinous results—an inrush of people, growths of towns, new social arrangements, gambling hells, demoralization, besides much wider effects—new businesses, new lines of traffic, and the changes presently caused throughout the world in the relative values of gold and goods.

The particular instance of this fructifying causa-

135

tion which I have now in view, dates back to a year
or two before the last General Election. Whether
Sir William Harcourt is a total abstainer, or whether
he was prompted by the miserable delusion that a
majority has unlimited right to control the acts of
individuals, or whether he thought that the support
of the teetotalers at the forthcoming election would
bring success, must remain undecided; but, for whatever reason, " local option " was made a " plank," as
the Americans say, in the Liberal platform. Considered from a tactical point of view the step was an
amazing one. During a year or more before the
election, I often commented on the impolicy of raising in every beer-house throughout the kingdom, a
pronounced antagonism. Not even in towns, and
still less in villages, did the mass of the electors care
a straw about Home Rule, which was to be the osten-
sible chief issue; but they cared greatly about the
threatened interference with the sale of beer. Every
urban publican had an interest in denouncing the proposed measure, and every rural publican, sympathizing with him, and fearing an extension of the interference, joined in the denunciations; while the fre-
quenters of their houses, threatened not only with
loss of their beer but with loss of their places of
resort, were willing listeners and joint denouncers.
The result, as we all know, was an overwhelming defeat of the party in power and a thrusting of them

aside by the opposition.   Of the multitudinous sequences of all kinds since witnessed, let me first indicate the most conspicuous set.

An ambitious man of despotic temper who, in the
Birmingham municipal government, had learned the
art of subordinating others, and had by ability and
audacity forced himself to the front in the central
government, became Colonial Secretary.   That his
determination to have his own way was the cause of
the still-progressing war in South Africa, no one now
doubts.   The results to the two republics have been
the loss of many thousands of lives, the breaking up
of multitudinous families, the destruction of countless
homesteads, the desolation of the country, the arrest
of industrial activities and complete social disorgan-
ization; while to ourselves the results have been the
deaths of some 25,000 soldiers on the battlefield and
in hospitals, as well as the invaliding of 60,000 others,
many of whom will die and others be maimed, the
immense increase of financial burdens by taxes and
loans, the checking of commercial activity, the kin-
dling of savage feelings causing brutal behaviour of
mobs, the rousing of hatred of us among Continental
peoples which will hereafter affect international relations, and the utter loss of that character for love
of freedom and sympathy with those who strive for it
which we before had.   These leading effects severally
ramify everywhere into unimaginable complications,
10

infinite in number, world-wide in reach, and heterogeneous in their kinds to an inconceivable degree;
and all of them were initiated by a small and utterly
irrelevant shibboleth. For had there been no thrusting of " local option " in the faces of electors, a possible defeat of the Liberal party, even had it occurred,
would not have given the antagonist party a majority
so enormous as to enable its leaders to do whatever
they pleased.*

But, as indicated above, numerous other sets of
important effects have followed the seemingly irrelevant cause. It is to these effects, and to the moral
to be drawn from them, that I would more especially
draw attention. Those in power, with the support
of their overwhelming majority, have, even avowedly, legislated in favour of their own class and of
the classes useful to them. By the Rating Acts of
1896 they relieved English and Scotch landowners to

---

* In addition to the general evidence that change of opinion
on the question of Home Rule was not the cause of the violent
party-reaction, there was the special evidence furnished by the
case of Sir William Harcourt himself. On the occasion of the
previous election he had been popular with the electors of Derby,
but at the election of 1895 he was hurled from his seat and a
Conservative put in his place (a rare thing for Derby, which has
almost invariably elected Liberals), and then at the recent election (1900), when the question of local option had been practically shelved, this Conservative was rejected and replaced by a
Liberal. The *animus* against Sir William Harcourt as the ex-
ponent of the teetotal crusade, could hardly have been more
clearly shown,

the extent of a million and a half; imposing that burden on other rate-payers.   In 1897 a " dole " of
£800,000 a year was given to the " denominational "
schools, advantaging them in their competition with
Board Schools and increasing the power of the
Church.   In the shape of relief from agricultural
rates, Ireland, and in considerable part the Irish landowners, were benefited to the extent of £727,000 a
year, and equivalent extra burdens were undertaken
by the State, that is, imposed on British taxpayers.
Once more in 1899, by the Clerical Tithes Act, ten
or eleven thousand incumbents were relieved from
half of the rates they had to pay on their tithe-rent
charge, and the community at large became responsible for that amount.   So that, passing over smaller
encroachments, those in office benefited their friends
to the amount of over £3,000,000, indirectly taken
from the pockets of the nation at large.   Power given
in support of a particular policy was used by the ministry to carry out other policies which would never
have been approved by the electors had they been
consulted.

    " Well, but what are we to do? " will be the ques-
tion asked.   " All these evils are the results of our
system of government, and we must make the best of
them.   We cannot avoid having parties.   An obedient majority will necessarily enable its leaders to do

things at variance with the wishes of those who put it
in power.   Only by the abolition of party-govern-
ment, which no one thinks possible, can this mischievous working out of things be changed."

I demur to this conclusion.   Were every member
of Parliament true to his convictions—did every one
resolve that he would not tell falsehoods by his votes
—did each cease to regard " party loyalty " as a vir-
tue, and decide to give effect to his unit of opinion,
regardless of ministerial interests—these over-ridings
of the national will by a few gentlemen in Downing
Street would be impossible.

" But such a course would bring government to
a deadlock," will be rejoined.   " No ministry could
continue in office for a month if it could not count
upon a body of supporters who would vote for its
measures whether they approved of them or not.
Ministry after ministry would be thrown out and public business arrested."

Here is one of those not infrequent cases in which
men discussing some proposed change, assume that
while the change is made other things remain unchanged; whereas it is always to be assumed that
other things will change simultaneously.   If representatives, or a large proportion of them, decided
that they would no longer by their votes say they believed things were good which they really believed
were bad; and if, while receiving adequate support

on certain main issues, the ministry was frequently left in a minority on minor issues, and, in conformity with the present practice, resigned; and if the like happened with subsequent ministries; it would presently be recognized as unfit that a government approved in its general conduct of affairs should resign because it was defeated—even often defeated—on subordinate questions: especially if those who usually supported it, but who were about to vote against it, announced that their dissent must not be taken as indicating any general dissatisfaction. Only in cases where the defeats of the ministry were frequent enough to show that its policy at large was condemned, would resignation be the sequence, and the appropriate sequence. In all ordinary cases ministers would simply accept the expression of dissent, and instead of resigning withdraw the offending measure.

And now observe what would be the general results. No longer able to pass measures disapproved by the opposition and by many of its own followers, a ministry would be able to pass only such measures as were approved by a majority of representatives of all parties—or rather, let us say, fragments of parties; and, by implication, would be able to pass only such measures as would probably be approved by most of the constituencies. A ministry which came into power to achieve one purpose willed by the country, would not be able subsequently to use its power to

achieve purposes not willed by the country but at
variance with its will.   That is to say, a ministry
would become that which its name implies, a servant,
instead of being what it is now, a master—a servant
not, as originally, of the monarch, but a servant of
the house and the nation.

At present that which we boast of as political
freedom consists in the ability to choose a despot or a
group of oligarchs, and after long misbehaviour has
produced dissatisfaction, to choose another despot or
group of oligarchs: having meanwhile been made subject to laws sundry of which are repugnant.   Abolish
the existing conventional usage—let each member
feel that he may express by his vote his adverse belief respecting a government measure, without en-
dangering the government's stability, and the whole
of this vicious system would disappear.   Constituencies through their representatives would really come
to be the makers of the laws they live under.

But what if each constituency has bound its representative to follow a party-leader?   Yes, here comes
the crux.   Political vices have their roots in the nature of the people.   The ability to find candidates
who will bind themselves to party-programmes, and
the wish to find such candidates, are alike indicative
of an average character not fitted for truly free institutions, but fitted only for those institutions under
which despotism is from time to time mitigated by

freedom. Freedom in its full sense—the power to
carry on the activities of life with no greater restric-
tions than those entailed by the claims of others to
like power—is understood by very few. Illustrations
of the current inability meet us on all sides. Men
who take shares in a company formed for a specified
purpose and then think themselves bound by the vote
of a two-thirds majority to undertake some other purpose, do not perceive that they are aggressed upon—
do not see that those who have entered into a contract
are not bound to do a thing which they have not con-
tracted to do, and that therefore they are wronged.
Ratepayers who elect members of a municipal government for the local maintenance of order, and for
certain public administrations, and then submit to be
taxed for purposes they never dreamt of (as subscribing capital for a canal) if a majority of the elected
body so decide, fail to understand the nature of liberty. Similarly those who, joining a trade-union,
surrender their freedom to make engagements on
their own terms, and allow themselves to be told by
their leaders when to work and when not to work,
have no adequate sense of that fundamental right
which every man possesses to make the best of himself, and to dispose of his abilities in any way he
pleases. Naturally, then, it results that those who
represent electors who are thus vague in their conceptions of freedom, and deficient in the accompany-

ing sentiment, must be expected to submit to party-dictates, and to say by their votes that they approve things which they do not approve. For the present there is no probability of anything better, but a probability of something worse; for the retrograde movement now going on towards the militant social type, is inevitably accompanied not by relaxation of authority but by enforcement of it.

EXAGGERATIONS AND MIS-STATEMENTS.

I HAVE read or heard that James Mill punished his daughters for bad reasoning. What penalties were inflicted I did not learn; but so drastic a method of dealing with defects of thought, which are in many cases due to incurable defects of nature, does not commend itself to me.

I should, however, be inclined to inflict on young people certain punishments for exaggerations and mis-statements—punishments having relevance to the offences and naturally serving to check them. In each instance a fit task would be to write out a correct definition of the misused word, followed by some examples of its appropriate use. The penalty would be slight and in all respects improving; since, besides impressing on the offender the meaning of the word, it would constitute an exercise in definition: there would be frequent discipline in exact thinking. Such discipline is ignored in the current conceptions of education, though immensely more important than much other discipline that is insisted on. Of course parallel kinds of penalties might be inflicted for mis-state-

145

ments—not mis-statements of things learned from books, but mis-statements of the incidents of daily life, private and public, which are conspicuous in the conversation of both young and old from hour to hour.

All are transgressors, and consequently all take lenient views of the transgression. Passing feelings prompt stronger words than are justifiable, and the desire to interest listeners increases perversions otherwise caused. I find that I am myself to be blamed for thus corrupting expression: discovering, as I often do when revising manuscript, that the word " very " had been used where it was uncalled for. From minute to minute every one utters needless adjectives and adverbs. We rarely hear anyone say he has a cold: it is nearly always a " bad " cold, or a " very bad " cold. If it be a question of weather, then a warm day in Spring is spoken of as " hot ": a description inapplicable save to days in July or August. Supposing it should rain moderately, it is said to be " pouring "—a word rightly used only in case of a thunder-shower or shower like it. Similarly, a little thin ice over the puddles is thought to justify the description " a hard frost." And if the question concerns the merit or demerit of a person or performance, he or it is represented as much above or much below the average. Conversation is thickly sprinkled with superlatives, and yet it needs but a moment's thought to see that superlatives should occur but rarely, since extreme cases bear but a small ratio to medium cases.

Criticisms passed on these licenses of speech are pooh-poohed or disregarded. It is forgotten that they are manifestations of a habit, and that while mostly little or no harm results, the habit occasionally results in harm that is serious. To say that exaggerations are of no consequence is to say that it matters not whether language conveys truth or error: partial and trivial error in most cases, but grave error in some cases. My attention has recently been drawn to the consequent evils by personal experiences, which show that words carelessly used, even in private letters, may, through a publication never dreamt of when they were written, cause mischiefs.

The first of the experiences to which I refer is supplied by *The Life and Letters of T. H. Huxley.* On page 333 of Vol. I, in a letter to his German friend Dr. Dohrn, jocosely threatening to pull to pieces some of his new ideas if he sends them, he, in illustration of his threat, refers to me in the following words— "I have been *his* devil's advocate for a number of years, and there is no telling how many brilliant speculations I have been the means of choking in an embryonic state." Interpreted with the aid of the context, this sentence will, by the critically-minded, not be taken seriously; but those who are not crit-

ically-minded, will give a literal meaning to the expression " no telling how many brilliant speculations,
&c." Feeling that, in the absence of correction, this
phrase would mislead, I requested my secretary (who
now writes to my dictation) to compare the original
MSS. with the printed books. He found that in the
two works, *First Principles* and *The Principles of
Biology*, occupying three volumes, which were seen
in proof by Prof. Huxley, there were four speculative
passages in the MSS. which had disappeared from the
printed text: one of them, however, having been
afterwards reproduced by me in an appendix, because
good warrant for it had become known. A further
misapprehension results. It was necessary that on my
biological writings I should have the criticisms of an
expert, and these were kindly given to me by Prof.
Huxley; but I did not ask his criticisms on my psychological, sociological, and ethical writings, nor on my
writings of a miscellaneous kind. Nevertheless certain other passages in Mr. Leonard Huxley's Life of
his father leave on most readers, if not on all, the impression that I received these. There is, on page 68
of Vol. II, a statement that he had been my " ' devil's
advocate ' for thirty-odd years " *—the whole period

---

* It is probable that Mr. Leonard Huxley, who published in
the *Athenæum* for Dec. 8, 1900, a letter making certain rectifica-
tions I pointed out as needful, has omitted from later editions
the passage containing these words.

of our friendship up to the date of the letter; and this, joined with mentions of proof-reading elsewhere, appears to imply that he read the proofs of the various works written during that time, and that in the absence of his restraining influence I should have published in them numerous ill-based speculations. This injurious implication, resulting from careless expressions, I cannot pass unrectified. Out of sixteen published volumes he saw the proofs of three only, to which must be added the proofs of some small fragments. That he was very apt in his letters to make statements of too sweeping a kind, the reader may himself find clear proof. On page 268 of Vol. II (first edition), speaking of use-inheritance, he writes —" Spencer is bound to it *a priori*—his psychology goes to pieces without it." Now anyone who turns to the first volume of *The Principles of Psychology*, and reads Parts I, II, and III, and then turns to the second volume and reads Parts VI and VII may see that his statement is quite misleading. It implies that were use-inheritance disproved the whole system would fall to the ground, whereas it is only in Parts IV and V that use-inheritance is implied; and some contend that even the changes described in these might be effected by natural selection. This proneness to over-statement was not limited to letters. Published writings exemplify it. The views which I hold respecting the limitation of State-functions he called "administrative nihilism"; though, beyond national defence, I hold it to be the business of the State to defend citizens not only from crimes of violence and aggression against one another but also from all civil injuries down to commission of nuisances (see *Essays*, Vol. II, p. 442).

The other instance to which I refer, while it in some measure illustrates the mischief done by exaggeration, also illustrates the mischief that may arise from indefiniteness. In a sketch of my career and works published by a warmly sympathetic narrator, there occurs this sentence:—" Like Aristotle, he has had to delegate large portions of his work to be done for him by others." Those who know that the work delegated by Aristotle was the collection of materials for his Natural History, will rightly interpret the reference. But not one reader in ten knows this, and hence wrong inferences will probably be drawn. As my name is especially associated with The Synthetic Philosophy, this sentence will suggest to many the thought that "large portions" of it were written by deputy. This he did not mean to say. The work to which he referred is entitled—" Descriptive Sociology; or Groups of Sociological Facts, classified and arranged by Herbert Spencer, compiled and abstracted by David Duncan, Richard Scheppig, and James Collier ": eight parts of which have thus far appeared. Knowing that I should be unable to read all the works of travel and history containing the facts I should need when dealing with the science of society, I engaged these gentlemen—first one, then two, then three—to read up for me, and arrange the extracts they made in the manner prescribed. With much material I had accumulated in the course of many years, I incorporated a much larger amount of material derived from these compilations when writing the *Principles of Sociology*, and Part II of the *Principles of Ethics*.

If even the sympathetic are apt to do mischief by misused words, what is to be expected from the antagonistic? Nobody needs telling that the effect of animosity of every kind, personal, political, theological, or philosophical, is greatly to intensify exaggerations and multiply mis-statements. I have had much experience in controversy, and speaking with strict regard to facts so far as I can recall them—avoiding carefully that exaggeration I am condemning—my impression is that in three cases out of four the alleged opinions of mine condemned by opponents, are not opinions of mine at all, but are opinions wrongly ascribed by them to me; sometimes from carelessness but more frequently from perversity: seeming, not unfrequently, to deliberate.

In illustration of the extent to which opposition, whether expressed in controversy or otherwise expressed, prompts injurious misrepresentations, I may

quote a passage from the *Letters of Benjamin Jowett*,
page 190:—

"I sometimes think that we Platonists and Idealists are
not half so industrious as those repulsive people who only 'believe what they can hold in their hands,' Bain, H. Spencer, etc.,
who are the very Tuppers of Philosophy."

I will not ask in what sense the Law of Evolution and
sundry generalizations of an abstract kind with which
I am identified, can be severally held in my hands,
but will interpret this statement in the sense probably intended, as an ascription of materialism.   One
might have expected that Prof. Jowett, learned in
philosophy and practised in making distinctions,
would not have followed in the steps of less cultured
theological opponents, whose aspersions I have time
after time shown to be groundless.   It might have
been supposed that since the System of Synthetic
Philosophy commences with a division entitled " The
Unknowable," having for its purpose to show that all
material phenomena are manifestations of a Power
which transcends our knowledge—that " force, as we
know it, can be regarded only as a conditioned effect
of the Unconditioned Cause " (§ 51), there had been
afforded sufficiently decided proof of belief in something which cannot be held in the hands.   Considering that in *The Principles of Psychology*, § 63, I have
written—" Hence though of the two it seems easier
to translate so-called Matter into so-called Spirit, than
to translate so-called Spirit into so-called Matter

(which latter is, indeed, wholly impossible), yet no translation can carry us beyond our symbols," I might reasonably have thought that no one would call me a materialist. Still more after the elaborate analysis contained in §§ 271, 272, showing the untenability of materialism; I should have supposed the repudiation complete. But the charge of materialism is a convenient weapon for theological and philosophical opponents—a weapon which, knocked out of the hand of one, is presently picked up by another—a weapon which Prof. Jowett was not ashamed to use and to join with vilifying words.*

---

* "But perhaps he did not know of these passages," some defender will say. I am not aware that one who condemns an author's opinions is excused because he does not know what those opinions are: rather his ignorance adds to the gravity of his offence. But the excuse, bad though it is, is unavailing, for Prof. Jowett had in his hands the works containing these passages. More than the first half of The Synthetic Philosophy was originally issued in portions of 80 pages to subscribers, who paid ten shillings for every four numbers. Prof. Jowett was among the original subscribers. When the series had been running for seven years, Prof. Jowett, annoyed, I suppose, at the trouble of having to pay ten shillings at intervals, sent to my publishers a lump sum of £5 to cover future subscriptions. On completion of the 44th number I decided to publish the remaining volumes in the ordinary way. At that time the £5 sent by Prof. Jowett was unexhausted, and the balance was sent back to him. Thus, beyond the fact that he was a subscriber from the beginning, there is the more remarkable fact that out of about four hundred original subscribers, he was the only one who paid subscriptions in advance—paid, in fact, ten subscriptions in advance.

In presence of the quotation which I have above given, these statements will be thought incredible: at any rate verification

11

Returning from these illustrations to the topic at large, let me insist more than thus far, on the enormous mischiefs which careless speech produces. Bloodshed, loss of life, national disaster, are in considerable measure traceable to it.   Passions, alike of individuals and of peoples, once aroused are intensified by vilifications, often unwarranted from the outset and beyond question unwarranted as the passions rise to their climax, and men, blinded by fury, utter any calumnies which come first into thought.   Of course

---

will be asked.   I therefore wrote to my publishers, thinking that though the subscription-book ceased to be used 22 years ago, there might yet be found, if not in it yet in some other book of accounts, a verifying entry.   This turned out to be true, as is shown by the following letter:—

14 Henrietta St., Covent Garden,
21 August, 1899.

Dear Sir,—

In answer to your letter of the 20th inst. it appears from the only book to which we can refer that Prof. Jowett paid to us the sum of £5 on 12 March, 1867, on account of Synthetic Philosophy, and that eventually the sum of £1 was returned to him. We regret that we cannot trace the date of this repayment, as we have not the cash-books or letters of that date.

We are, &c.,
WILLIAMS & NORGATE.

Here, then, is a psychological puzzle.   Prof. Jowett's practical proof of approbation was inversely proportionate to his expressed disapprobation!   While showing, in an extremely exceptional way, if not his agreement with the Synthetic Philosophy yet his appreciation of it, he described its author as an "empty sciolist" [words used in another passage].   Prof. Jowett was said to be difficult to understand.   Here is a problem for his admirers which they will, I think, not easily solve.

the great mass of the English people will refuse to see that our reckless exaggerations and reckless mis-statements, have been in large measure to blame for the evils we are ourselves now suffering while inflicting greater evils on others; but they will not refuse to see that exaggerations and mis-statements have immensely increased the hatred now felt for England by Continental nations.   They must surely perceive that this universal misuse of language is at the present moment a source of international danger; since, while the French and the Germans are anxious to find excuses for fighting us, small incidents may precipitate disastrous wars.   Obviously the animosity lately generated, which, as I hear from a German friend especially characterizes the young, may hereafter be a cause of wholesale slaughter, resurgence of savagery, and vast financial burdens.   Hence it is a duty to reprobate habits of exaggeration.   I say habits, because if words are misused in small and indifferent matters they will be misused in great and important ones.   It is folly to suppose that those who, when trivialities are in question, use stronger words than are called for, will suddenly become judicial in their speech when the things discussed are momentous.

" So then we are to make our talk prim and exact and consequently dull: looking at our words before we utter them to see that they do not go beyond the truth? Why, were that done, conversation would lose all its salt!" Such is the kind of response to be expected from those who exaggerate and who defend exaggeration. The response comes appropriately, since it illustrates that randomness of thought which exaggeration itself does. The implication of the above argument is that words which truly express the facts should be used in all cases where the obvious intention is to express facts; not at all that words should be used in this way when there is an obvious intention to overstate with a view to cause amusement. Humorous exaggeration would be increased in effect when it came from the mouth of one who ordinarily used words appropriately.

IMPERIALISM AND SLAVERY.

" You shall submit. We are masters and we will
make you acknowledge it! " These words express
the sentiment which sways the British nation in its
dealings with the Boer republics; and this sentiment
it is which, definitely displayed in this case, pervades
indefinitely the political feeling now manifesting itself as Imperialism. Supremacy, where not clearly
imagined, is vaguely present in the background of
consciousness. Not the derivation of the word only,
but all its uses and associations, imply the thought
of predominance—imply a correlative subordination.
Actual or potential coercion of others, individuals or
communities, is necessarily involved in the conception.

There are those, and unhappily they form the
great majority, who think there is something noble
(morally as well as historically) in the exercise of
command—in the forcing of others to abandon their
own wills and fulfil the will of the commander. I
am not about to contest this sentiment. I merely
say that there are others, unhappily but few, who

think it ignoble to bring their fellow creatures into
subjection, and who think the noble thing is not only
to respect their freedom but also to defend it. Leaving this matter undiscussed, my present purpose is to
show those who lean towards Imperialism, that the
exercise of mastery inevitably entails on the master
himself some form of slavery, more or less pronounced. The uncultured masses, and even the
greater part of the cultured, will regard this statement as absurd; and though many who have read
history with an eye to essentials rather than trivialities know that this is a paradox in the right sense—
that is, true in fact though not seeming true—even
they are not fully conscious of the mass of evidence
establishing it, and will be all the better for having
illustrations recalled. Let me begin with the earliest
and simplest, which well serves to symbolize the
whole.

Here is a prisoner with hands tied and a cord
round his neck (as suggested by figures in Assyrian
bas-reliefs) being led home by his savage conqueror,
who intends to make him a slave. The one, you say,
is captive and the other free? Are you quite sure
the other is free? He holds one end of the cord, and
unless he means to let his captive escape, he must continue to be fastened by keeping hold of the cord in
such way that it cannot easily be detached. He must
be himself tied to the captive while the captive is

tied to him. In other ways his activities are impeded
and certain burdens are imposed on him. A wild
animal crosses the track, and he cannot pursue. If
he wishes to drink of the adjacent stream, he must
tie up his captive lest advantage be taken of his de-
fenceless position. Moreover he has to provide food
for both. In various ways, then, he is no longer completely at liberty; and these ways adumbrate in a
simple manner the universal truth that the instru-
mentalities by which the subordination of others is
effected, themselves subordinate the victor, the master, or the ruler.

The coincidence in time between the South African war and the recent outburst of Imperialism, illustrates the general truth that militancy and Imperialism are closely allied—are, in fact, different manifestations of the same social condition. It could not,
indeed, be otherwise. Subject races or subject societies, do not voluntarily submit themselves to a ruling
race or a ruling society: their subjection is nearly always the effect of coercion. An army is the agency
which achieved it, and an army must be kept ever
ready to maintain it. Unless the supremacy has
actual or potential force behind it there is only fed-
eration, not Imperialism. Here, however, as above
implied, the purpose is not so much to show that an
imperial society is necessarily a militant society, as
to show that in proportion as liberty is diminished

in the societies over which it rules, liberty is diminished within its own organization.

The earliest records furnish an illustration. Whether in the times of the pyramid-builders the power of the Egyptian autocrat, which effected such astounding results, was qualified by an elaborate system of restraints, we have no evidence; but there is proof that in later days he was the slave of the governmental organization.

> "The laws subjected every action of his private life to as severe a scrutiny as his behaviour in the administration of affairs. The hours of washing, walking, and all the amusements and occupations of the day, were settled with precision, and the quantity as well as the quality of his food were regulated by law." (*Manners and Customs of the Ancient Egyptians*, Birch's ed. of Wilkinson, vol. I, 166.)

Moreover the relation between enslavement of foreign peoples and enslavement of the nation which conquered them, is shown by an inscription at Karnak, which describes "how bitterly the country was paying the price of its foreign conquests, in its oppression by its standing army." (Flinders Petrie, *History of Egypt*, ii. 252.)

Turn we now to a society of widely different type but exhibiting the same general truths—that of Sparta. The conquering race, or Spartans proper, who had beneath them the Periœci and the Helots, descendants of two subject races, were not only supreme over these but twice became the supreme race

of the Peleponnesus. What was the price they paid
for their "imperial" position? The individual Spar-
tan, master as he was over slaves and semi-slaves, was
himself in bondage to the incorporated society of
Spartans. Each led the life not which he himself
chose but the life dictated by the aggregate of which
he formed one unit. And this life was a life of
strenuous discipline, leaving no space for culture, or
art, or poetry, or other source of pleasure. He exemplified in an extreme degree the Grecian doctrine
that the citizen does not belong to himself or to his
family but to his city.

If instead of the small and simple community of
Sparta we take the vast and complex empire of Rome,
we find this essential connexion between imperialism
and slavery even more conspicuous. I do not refer
to the fact that three-fourths of those who peopled
Italy in imperial days were slaves, chained in the
fields when at work, chained at night in their dormi-
tories, and those who were porters chained to the
doorways—conditions horrible to contemplate—but
I refer to the fact that the nominally free part of
the community consisted of grades of bondmen. Not
only did citizens stand in that bondage implied by
military service, complete or partial, under subjection
so rigid that an officer was to be dreaded more than
an enemy, but those occupied in civil or semi-civil
life, were compelled to work for the public. " Every-

one was treated in fact as a servant of the State . . . the nature of each man's labour was permanently fixed for him." The society was formed of fighting serfs, working serfs, cultivating serfs, official serfs. And then what of the supreme head of this gigantic bureaucracy into which Roman society had grown—the Emperor? He became a puppet of the Pretorian guard, which while a means of safety was a cause of danger. Moreover he was in daily bondage to routine. As Gibbon says, " the emperor was the first slave of the ceremonies he imposed." Thus in a conspicuous manner Rome shows how, as in other cases, a society which enslaves other societies enslaves itself.

The same lesson is taught by those ages of seething confusion—of violence and bloodshed—which the collapse of the Roman empire left: an empire which dwells in the minds of the many as something to be admired and emulated—the many who forgive any horrors if only their brute love of mastery is gratified, sympathetically when not actually. Passing over those sanguinary times in which the crimes of Clovis and Fredegonde and Brunehaut were typical, we come in the slow course of things to the emergence of the feudal régime—a régime briefly expressed by the four words, suzerains, vassals, serfs, slaves—a régime which, along with the perpetual struggles for supremacy among local rulers, and consequent chronic militancy, was characterized by the unqualified power of each chief or ruler, count or duke, within his own territory—a graduated bondage of all below him. The established form—" I am your man," uttered by the vassal on his knees with apposed hands, expressed the relation of one grade to another throughout the society; and then, as usual, the master of slaves was himself enslaved by his appliances for maintaining life and power. He had the perpetual burden of arms and coat of mail, and the precautions to be taken now against assassination now against death by poison. And then when we come to the ultimate state in which the subordination of minor rulers by a chief ruler had become complete, and all counts and dukes were vassals of the king, we have not only the bondage entailed on the king by State-business with its unceasing anxieties, but the bondage of ceremonial with its dreary round. Speaking of this in France in the time of Louis le Grand, Madame de Maintenon remarks—" Save those only who fill the highest stations, I know of none more unfortunate than those who envy them. If you could only form an idea of what it is! "

Merely referring to the extreme subjection of the ruler to his appliances for ruling which was reached in Japan, where the god-descended Mikado, imprisoned by the requirements of his sacred state, was debarred from ordinary freedoms, and in whose re-

cluse life there were at one time such penalties as
sitting for three hours daily on the throne—passing
over, too, the case of China, where, as Prof. Douglas
tells us of the emperor " his whole life is one continual round of ceremonial observances," and " from
the day on which he ascends the throne to the time
when he is carried to his tomb in the Eastern Hills,
his hours and almost minutes have special duties appointed to them by the Board of Rites "; we may
turn now to the conspicuous example furnished by
Russia. Along with that unceasing subjugation of
minor nationalities by which its imperialism is displayed, what do we see within its own organization?
We have its vast army, to service in which every one
is actually or potentially liable; we have an enormous bureaucracy ramifying everywhere and rigidly
controlling individual lives; we have an expenditure
ever outrunning resources and calling for loans. As
a result of the pressure felt personally and pecunia-
rily, we have secret revolutionary societies, perpetual
plots, chronic dread of social explosions; and while
everyone is in danger of Siberia, we have the all-
powerful head of this enslaved nation in constant fear
for his life. Even when he goes to review his troops,
rigorous precautions have to be taken by a supple-
mentary army of soldiers, policemen, and spies, some
forming an accompanying guard, some lying in wait
here and there to prevent possible attacks; while sim-

ilar precautions, which from time to time fail, have ever to be taken against assassination by explosion, during drives and railway-journeys. What portion of life is not absorbed in government-business and religious observances is taken up in self-preservation.

And now what is the lesson? Is it that in our own case imperialism and slavery, everywhere else and at all times united, are not to be united? Most will say Yes. Nay they will join, as our Poet Laureate lately did in the title to some rhymes, the words " Imperialism and Liberty "; mistaking names for things as of old.   Gibbon writes:—

"Augustus was sensible that mankind is governed by names; nor was he deceived in his expectation, that the senate and people would submit to slavery, provided they were respectfully assured that they still enjoyed their ancient freedom." (*Decline and Fall,* i. 68.)

" Free! " thinks the Englishman, " How can I be other than free if by my vote I share in electing a representative who helps to determine the national transactions, home and foreign? " Delivering a ballot-paper he identifies with the possession of those unrestrained activities which liberty implies; though, to take but one instance, a threatened penalty every day reminds him that his children must be stamped with the State-pattern, not as he wills but as others will.

But let us note how, along with the nominal ex-

tension of constitutional freedom, there has been
going on actual diminution of it. There is first the
fact that the legislative functions of Parliament have
been decreasing while the Ministry has been usurping them. Important measures are not now brought
forward and carried by private members, but appeal
is made to the government to take them up: the
making of laws is gradually lapsing into the hands
of the executive. And then within the executive itself the tendency is towards placing power in fewer
hands. Just as in past times the Cabinet grew out
of the Privy Council by a process of restriction, so
now a smaller group of ministers is coming to exercise some of the functions of the whole group. Add
to which we have subordinate executive bodies, like
the Home Office, the Board of Trade, the Board of
Education, and the Local Government Board, to
which there have been deputed the powers both of
making certain kinds of laws and enforcing them:
government by administrative order. In like manner by taking for government-purposes more and
more of the time which was once available for private
members; by the cutting down of debates by the closure; and now by requiring the vote for an entire
department to be passed *en bloc*, without criticism of
details; we are shown that while extension of the
franchise has been seeming to increase the liberties
of citizens, their liberties have been decreased by

restricting the spheres of action of their representatives. All these are stages in that concentration of
power which is the concomitant of Imperialism.*
And how this tendency works out where militancy
becomes active, we are shown by the measures taken
in South Africa—the proclamation of martial law
by a governor, who thereby becomes in so far a
despot, and the temporary suspension of constitutional government: a suspension which many so-
called loyalists would make complete.

Passing by this, however, let us note the extent
to which the citizen is the servant of the community
in disguised ways. Certain ancient usages will best
make this clear. During times when complete slavery was mingled with serfdom, the serf, tied to his
plot, rendered to his lord or seigneur many dues and
services. These services, or *corvées*, varied, according
to the period and the place, from one day's labour
to six days' labour in the week—from partial slavery
to complete slavery. Labours and exactions of these
kinds were most of them in course of time commuted
for money: the equivalence between so much tax paid
to the lord and so much work done for him, being
thus distinctly recognized. Now in so far as the
burden is concerned, it comes to the same thing if for

---

* Even while I have the proof in my hands there come the
new rules of procedure, further diminishing the freedom of members.

the feudal lord we substitute the central government, and for local money-payments we substitute general taxes. The essential question for the citizen is what part of his work goes to the power which rules over him, and what part remains available for satisfying his own wants. Labour demanded by the State is just as much *corvée* to the State as labour demanded by the feudal lord was *corvée* to him, though it may not be called so, and though it may be given in money instead of in kind; and to the extent of this *corvée* each citizen is a serf to the community. Some five years ago M. Guyot calculated that in France, the civil and military expenditure absorbs some 30 per cent. of the national produce, or, in other words, that 90 days annually of the average citizen's labour is given to the State under compulsion.

Though to a smaller extent, what holds in France holds here. Not forgetting the heavy burden of State-*corvées* which the Imperialism of past days bequeathed to us—the 150 millions of debt incurred for the American war and the 50 millions we took over with the East India Company's possessions, the interest on both of which entails on citizens extra labour annually, let us limit ourselves to the burdens Imperialism now commits us to. From a statistical authority second to none, I learn that 100 millions of annual expenditure requires from the average citizen the labour of one day in every seven-

teen, that is to say, nearly eighteen days in the year.
As the present permanent expenditure on army and
navy plus the interest on the debt recently con-
tracted amounts to about 76 millions, it results that
13½ days' labour per annum is thus imposed on the
average citizen as *corvée*. And then there comes the
£153,000,000 spent, and to be spent, on the South
African and Chinese wars, to which may be added,
for all subsequent costs of pensions, repairs, compensations, and re-instatements, a sum which will raise
the total to more than £200,000,000. What is the
taxation which direct expenditure and interest on
loans will entail, the reader may calculate. He has
before him the data for an estimate of the extra
number of days annually, during which Imperialism
will require him to work for the Government—extra
number, I say, because to meet the ordinary State-
expenditure, there must always be a large number
of days spent by him as a State-labourer. Doubtless
one who is satisfied by names instead of things, as
the Romans were, will think this statement absurd;
but he who understands by freedom the ability to use
his powers for his own ends, with no greater hindrance
than is implied by the like ability of each other citizen, will see that in whatever disguised ways he is
obliged to use his abilities for State-purposes, he is to
that extent a serf of the State; and that as fast as
our growing Imperialism augments the amount of
12

such compulsory service, he is to that extent more
and more a serf of the State.

And then beyond the roundabout services given
by the citizen under the form of direct taxes and
under the form of indirect taxes, severally equivalent to so many days' work that would else have elevated the lives of himself and his belongings, there
will presently come the actual or potential service
as a soldier, demanded by the State to carry out an
imperialist policy—a service which, as those in South
Africa can tell us, often inflicts under the guise of
fine names a slavery harder than that which the negro
bears, with the added risk of death.

Even were it possible to bring home to men the
extent to which their lives are, and presently will be
still more, subordinated to State-requirements, so as
to leave them less and less owned by themselves, little
effect would be produced. So long as the passion for
mastery overrides all others the slavery that goes
along with Imperialism will be tolerated. Among
men who do not pride themselves on the possession
of purely human traits, but on the possession of traits
which they have in common with brutes, and in whose
mouths " bull-dog courage " is equivalent to manhood
—among people who take their point of honour from
the prize-ring, in which the combatant submits to
pain, injury, and risk of death, in the determination
to prove himself " the better man," no deterrent con-

siderations like the above will have any weight. So long as they continue to conquer other peoples and to hold them in subjection, they will readily merge their personal liberties in the power of the State, and hereafter as heretofore accept the slavery that goes along with Imperialism.

RE–BARBARIZATION.

ALL societies, be they those savage tribes which have acquired some political structure or those nations which have grown vast by conquering adjacent nations, show that, as said above, the cardinal trait of fighting peoples is the subjection of man to man and of group to group. Graduated subordination, which is the method of army-organization, becomes more and more the method of civil organization where militancy is chronic; since where militancy is chronic, the civil part becomes little else than a commissariat supplying the wants of the militant part, and is more and more subject to the same discipline. Further, familiar facts prove that emergence from those barbaric types of society evolved by chronic militancy, brings with it a decrease of this graduated subordination, and there results, as recent centuries have shown, an increase of freedom. To which let it be added that where, as among ourselves, the militant activities have for ages been less marked and the militant organization less pronounced, the growth of free institutions begins earlier and advances further.

172

An obvious corollary is that a cardinal trait in the process of re-barbarization is the re-growth of graduated subordination. Let us contemplate the facts.

The United States furnishes a fit looking-glass. Since the days when there grew up local " bosses " to whom clusters of voters were obedient, there has been a development of " bosses " whose authorities extend over wider areas; until now men of the type of Platt, and Hanna, and Croker mainly determine the elections, municipal and central. Conventions formed of delegates supposed to represent the wills of their respective localities, have become bodies which merely register the decisions of certain heads who nominally advise but practically dictate. And so completely has this system submerged the traditions of individual freedom, that now the assertion of such freedom has become a discredit, and the independent citizen, here and there found, who will not surrender his right of private judgment, bears the contemptuous name of " mugwump."

In England the Caucus, not yet supreme over the individual, has still in large measure deprived him of what electoral freedom he had during the generation following the Reform Bill; when, as I know from personal experience, the initiative of each citizen (even a non-elector) was of some effect. Now, governing bodies in each constituency undertake to judge for all members of their respective parties, who are obliged to accept the candidates chosen for them. Practically these bodies have become electoral oligarchies. Similarly in the House of Commons itself, this retrogressive movement, shown in ways described some pages back, is shown in further ways. There is the change which a few years ago cut off " the privilege of ventilating grievances before going into Committee of Supply "—cut off that which was the primary privilege of burgesses sent up from their respective constituencies in early days; since, on the rectification or mitigation of grievances, partially depended the granting of supplies. And then, recently, a kindred resolution has negatived the right of moving amendments to the motion for going into Committee of Ways and Means. Retrogression is thus shown by increasingly subordinating the citizen, alike as elector and as representative.

Ecclesiastical movements now going on, show us a kindred change. There is a return towards that subjection to a priesthood characteristic of barbaric types of Society. Rebellion of the Church against the civil power, is an indication of desire for that social régime which once made kings subject to the Pope. Throughout the hierarchy the strengthening of sacerdotalism is the aim, secret if not avowed; and the heads of the hierarchy when asked to put a check on those practices which assimilate the Church of England to the Church of Rome, evade and shuffle in such ways as to let them go on, while they are energetic in resisting efforts to prevent the assimilation. For a generation past there have been endeavours to mark off the priesthood as a body of intermediaries between God and man. Confession, the performance of a quasi-mass, and various ceremonies with incense accompaniment, have tended more and more to elevate the clerical class: the effects being re-inforced by gorgeous robes and jewelled symbols, such as were common in mediæval days and are akin to those of barbaric peoples at large.

For the changes which have thus been spreading throughout our social organization, political and religious, there have been several causes. The initial one was the setting up of that modest defensive organization, well justified under the circumstances, known originally as the Volunteer movement. When, by his policy, Louis Napoleon made it doubtful whether he had not in view an invasion of England, there arose something like a cry " To arms! " embodied by the Poet Laureate in his verses " Form, riflemen, form." There resulted, and thereafter continually grew, a body of civilians who were weekly subjected to drill and weekly exercised themselves in rifle shooting: both processes awakening in them the slumbering militant ideas and sentiments which have come down to us from early ages of perpetual warfare. The formation into companies and regiments, the passing through regular evolutions, the subjection to officers, the marching through the streets after their bands, joined with ambitions to occupy posts of command, cultivated in the young men of our towns the thoughts and emotions appropriate to fighting. A revived interest in war necessarily resulted; and the partially dormant instincts of the savage, readily aroused, have been exercising themselves if not on actual foes then on foes conceived to be invading us.

For these twenty years there has been at work another widespread cause, which few will at first recognize as a cause, but the effects of which analysis will make clear. The quality of a passion is in great measure the same whatever the object exciting it. Fear aroused by a mad dog is at the core like the fear produced by the raised weapon of an assassin; and the hate felt for a disgusting animal is of the same nature as the hate felt for a man very much disliked. Especially when the objects which excite the passions are imaginary, is there likely to be little difference between the states of mind produced. The cultivation of animosity towards one imaginary object, strengthening the sentiment of animosity at large, makes it easier to arouse animosity towards another imaginary object.

I make these remarks à propos of the Salvation Army. The word is significant—Army; as are the

names for the ranks, from the so-called " General,"
descending through brigadiers, colonels, majors,
down to local sub-officers, all wearing uniforms.
This system is like in idea and in sentiment to that
of an actual army. Then what are the feelings appealed to? The " Official Gazette of the Salvation
Army " is entitled *The War Cry;* and the motto conspicuous on the title-page is " Blood and Fire."
Doubtless it will be said that it is towards the principle of evil, personal or impersonal—towards " the
devil and all his works "—that the destructive sentiments are invoked by this title and this motto. So
it will be said that in a hymn, conspicuous in the
number of the paper I have in hand, the like *animus*
is displayed by the expressions which I cull from
the first thirty lines:—" Made us warriors for ever,
Sent us in the field to fight . . . We shall win with
fire and blood . . . Stand to your arms, the foe is
nigh, The powers of hell surround . . . The day of
battle is at hand! Go forth to glorious war." These
and others like them are stimuli to the fighting pro-
pensities, and the excitements of song joined with
martial processions and instrumental music cannot
fail to raise high those slumbering passions which
are ready enough to burst out even in the intercourse
of ordinary life. Such appeals as there may be to
the gentler sentiments which the creed inculcates,
are practically lost amid these loud-voiced invoca-

tions. Out of mixed and contradictory exhortations
the people who listen respond to those which are most
congruous with their own natures and are little affected by the rest; so that under the nominal forms
of the religion of amity there are daily exercised the
feelings appropriate to the religion of enmity. And
then, as before suggested, these destructive passions
directed towards "the enemy," as the principle of
evil is called, are easily directed towards an enemy
otherwise conceived. If for wicked spirits are sub-
stituted wicked men, these are regarded with the same
feelings; and when calumnies sown broadcast make
it appear that certain people are wicked men, the
anger and hate which have been perpetually fostered
are vented upon them.

Verifying facts are pointed out to me even while
I dictate, showing that not in the Salvation Army
alone but in the Church-services held on the occasion of the departure of troops for South Africa,
certain hymns are used in a manner which substitutes
for the spiritual enemy the human enemy. Thus for
a generation past, under cover of the forms of a
religion which preaches peace, love, and forgiveness,
there has been a perpetual shouting of the words
"war" and "blood," "fire" and "battle," and a continual exercise of the antagonistic feelings.

This diffusion of military ideas, military sentiments, military organization, military discipline, has

been going on everywhere. There is the competing body, the Church Army, which, not particularly obtrusive, we may presume from its name follows similar lines; and there is, showing more clearly the ecclesiastical bias in the same direction, the Church Lads' Brigade, with its uniform, arms, and drill. In these as in other things the clerical and the military are in full sympathy. The Rev. Dr. Warre, head master of Eton, reads a paper at the United Service Institution, arguing that in the public secondary schools there should be diffusion of the elements of military science, as well as exercise in military drill, manœuvres, use of fire-arms, &c. So, too, another head master, the Rev. Mr. Gull, in a lecture to the College of Preceptors under chairmanship of the Rev. Mr. Bevan, tells us that there are 79 cadet-corps in various public schools; that efforts are being made to " organize drill in elementary schools and for boys in the lower ranks of life "; that a committee of the Head Masters' Conference resolved unanimously that in public secondary schools boys over 15 should receive military drill and instruction; and that, by the suggestion of these " reverend " head masters, a Military Instruction Bill, embodying their views and favoured by the War Office, has been brought before both Houses of Parliament.* Similarly during the Guthrie Commemoration at Clifton

---

* See *Educational Times*, June 1, 1901.

College, the head master, the Rev. Canon Glaze-
brook, in presence of two bishops, glorified the part
which those educated at Clifton had taken in the
South African War: enlarging with pride on "so
noble a contribution in such a patriotic cause" as
the nineteen old Cliftonians who had fallen; dilating,
too, on the increasing zeal of the school in military
matters.   And now at Cambridge the Senate urges
that the University should take steps towards the
organization of instruction in military sciences.

More conspicuous growths of like nature have
taken place.   We have the reviews, manœuvres, and
training-camps of the Volunteers, and the annual
rifle-competitions now at Wimbledon now at Bisley;
we have the permanent camps at Shorncliffe and Al-
dershot, and are about to have a much larger one
on Salisbury Plain.   Fifty years ago we had no such
incidents as the "passages of arms" or tournaments
now held periodically, nor had we any military and
naval exhibitions.   Lastly, showing the utter change
of social sentiment, it was resolved at a Mansion
House meeting that the Great Exhibition of 1851,
which was expected to inaugurate universal peace,
should be commemorated in 1901 by a Naval and
Military Exhibition: an anti-militant display having
for its jubilee a militant display!

The temper generated by these causes has resulted in the outbursts of violence occurring all over

England in thirty towns large and small, where those who entertain opinions disliked by the majority respecting our treatment of the Boers, have been made the victims of mobs—mobs which not only suppressed even private meetings and ill-treated those who proposed to take part in them, kicking and even tarring them in the public streets, but attacked the premises of those who were known to be against the war, smashing shop-windows, breaking into houses, and even firing into them. And now after these breaches of the law, continued for two years, have been habitually condoned by the authorities, we find leading newspapers applauding the police for having " judiciously refrained " from interfering with a mob in its ill-treatment of Stop-the-War speakers! Surely a society thus characterized and thus governed is a fit habitat for Hooligans.

Naturally along with this exaltation of brute force in its armed form, as seen in military organizations, secular and sacred, as well as in the devotion of teaching institutions to fostering it, and along with these manifestations of popular passion, showing how widely the trait of coerciveness, which is the essential element in militancy, has pervaded the nation, there has gone a cultivation of skilled physical force under the form of athleticism. The word is quite modern, for the reason that a generation ago the facts to be embraced under it were not sufficiently numer-

ous and conspicuous to call for it. In my early days
" sports," so called, were almost exclusively represented by one weekly paper, *Bell's Life in London*,
found I am told in the haunts of rowdies and in
taverns of a low class. Since then, the growth has
been such that the acquirement of skill in leading
games has become an absorbing occupation. The
cricket-matches of local clubs are topics of interest
not only in their localities but elsewhere, and the
names of celebrated players are in the mouths of
multitudes. There are professionals and there are
courses of training; so that what was originally a
game has become a business. Similarly with rowing,
which has its competitions on all rivers large enough,
and its set matches, of which those between the Universities and those at Henley have become national
events, drawing enormous crowds, as does also the
Universities' cricket-match. And then football, in
my boyhood occupying no public attention, has now
provision made for it in every locality, and its leading contests between paid players, draw their tens of
thousands of spectators—nay even, as at Sydenham
lately, a hundred thousand spectators—whose natures
are such that police are often required for the protection of umpires. It may, indeed, be remarked
that this game, which has now become the most popular, is also the most brutalizing; for the merciless
struggles among the players, and the intensity of their

antagonisms, prove, even without the frequent in-
flictions of injuries and occasional deaths, that the
game approaches as nearly to a fight as lack of weapons allows.

"Sports" of past times, which law had forbidden
because of their brutality, are re-appearing. Occasionally one reads of secret cock-fights discovered by
the police and stopped; and now, in the resuscitated
periodical of Johnson, *The Rambler*, there is a deliberate advocacy of cock-fighting as an amusement. Of
like meaning is the revival of pugilism: the illegal
prize-fights having been replaced by so-called "glove-
fights," differing but nominally. Though within
these few years four deaths have resulted, yet such
is the sympathy of the authorities with the "sport,"
so called, that the manslaughters have on one or other
plea been in every case condoned. Along with this
development of human athletics has gone a development of animal athletics, or racing, under the form
of increase in the number of race-meetings; and both
kinds have been accompanied by an immense extension of betting and gambling—vices pervading all
classes and all places, from fashionable drawing-rooms
down to slums—vices furthering re-barbarization,
since pleasures obtained at the cost of pains to others,
necessarily entail a searing of the sympathies.

Meanwhile, to satisfy the demand journalism has
been developing, so that besides sundry daily and

weekly papers devoted wholly to sports, the ordinary daily and weekly papers give reports of " events " in all localities, and not unfrequently a daily paper has a whole page occupied with them. A grave concomitant is to be noted. While bodily superiority is coming to the front, mental superiority is retreating into the background. It has long been remarked that a noted athlete is more honoured than a student who has come out highest from the examinations; and if there needs ocular proof we have it in the illustrated papers, which continually reproduce photographs of competing crews and competing teams, while nowhere do we see a photograph of, say, all the wranglers of the year. How extreme is this predominance of athleticism is shown by the fact that Sir Michael Foster, when a candidate for the representation of the University of London, was described as specially fitted because he was a good cricketer! " All cricketers will, of course, vote for him," wrote in *The Times* a B.A. who had " played in the same eleven with him." Thus various changes point back to those mediæval days when courage and bodily power were the sole qualifications of the ruling classes, while such culture as existed was confined to priests and the inmates of monasteries.

Literature, journalism, and art, have all been aiding in this process of re-barbarization. For a long time there have flourished novel-writers who have rung the changes on narratives of crime and stories of sanguinary deeds. Others have been supplying boys and youths with tales full of plotting and fighting and bloodshed: millions of such having of late years been circulated;* and there have been numerous volumes of travel in which encounters with natives and the killing of big game have been the advertised attractions. Various war-books have followed in the wake of Prof. Creasy's *Fifteen Decisive Battles of the World* with its thirty-odd editions; and now, in the current number of the *Athenæum*, I see noted as forthcoming two works of this genus—the one, *Great Battles of the World*, and the other *All the World's Fighting Ships* for 1901, an annual publication. As indicating most clearly the state of national feeling, we have the immense popularity of Mr. Rudyard Kipling, in whose writings one-tenth of nominal Christianity is joined with nine-tenths of real paganism; who idealizes the soldier and glories in the triumphs of brute force; and who, in depicting school-life, brings to the front the barbarizing activities and feelings and shows little respect for a civilizing culture.

So, too, the literature of the periodicals reeks with violence. In the American magazines having wide English circulations, there went on, even before the recent conquests, *rechauffé* narratives of the Civil

---

* See *Academy*, June 5, 1897.

13

War—accounts of this or the other part of the campaign and biographies of this or the other leader.
Not content with battles and great captains of recent
times, editors have, to satisfy the appetites of readers, gone back to the remote past as well as to the
near past. The life and conquests of Alexander the
Great have been set forth afresh with illustrations;
and in serial articles, as also in book form, Napoleon
has again served as a subject for biography: Welling-
ton and Nelson too, have been resuscitated. Nay,
even memoirs of celebrated pirates and privateers
have been exhumed to meet the demand. At the
same time the fiction filling our monthly magazines,
has been mainly sanguinary. Tales of crimes and
deeds of violence, drawings of men fighting, men
overpowered, men escaping, of daggers raised, pis-
tols levelled—these, in all varieties of combination,
have appealed to our latent savagery. Among other
stories of this class there were recently two in each
of which the attraction was a prize-fight, made pi-
quant by wood-cuts. So has it been with our pictorial newspapers. Even before the recent wars there
were ever found occasions for representing bloody
combats, or else the appliances of destruction naval
and military, or else the leading men using them.
I suppose that of late such scenes and portraits have
been more numerous still—I say I suppose, because
for years past, disgusted with these stimuli to brutal-

ity, I have deliberately avoided looking at the illustrated weekly journals.

Thus on every side we see the ideas and feelings and institutions appropriate to peaceful life, replaced by those appropriate to fighting life. The continual increases of the army, the formation of permanent camps, the institution of public military contests and military exhibitions, have conduced to this result. The drills, and displays, and competitions, of civilian soldiers (not uncalled for when they began) have gone on exercising the combative feelings. Perpetual excitements of the destructive passions which, in the *War Cry* and in the hymns of General Booth's followers, have made battle and blood and fire familiar, and under the guise of fighting against evil have thrust into the background the gentler emotions, have done the like. Similarly in schools, military organization and discipline have been cultivating the instinct of antagonism in each rising generation. More and more the spirit of conflict has been exercised by athletic games, interest in which has been actively fostered first by the weekly Press and now by the daily Press; and with increase of the honours given to physical prowess there has been decrease of the honours given to mental prowess. Meanwhile literature and art have been aiding. Books treating of battles, conquests, and the men who conducted them, have been widely diffused and greedily read. Periodicals full of stories made interesting by killing, with accompanying illustrations, have every month ministered to the love of destruction; as have, too, the weekly illustrated journals. In all places and in all ways there has been going on during the past fifty years a recrudescence of barbaric ambitions, ideas and sentiments and an unceasing culture of blood-thirst.

If there needs a striking illustration of the result, we have it in the *dictum* of the people's Laureate, that the "lordliest life on earth" is one spent in seeking to "bag" certain of our fellow-men!

REGIMENTATION.

At first sight the title "Regimentation" seems to imply nothing more than a description in detail of the changes set forth above; but while in part it brings into view one side of these changes, and suggests their common tendency, it serves a further end. I use it here to express certain wider changes which are their concomitants. For as indicated some pages back, and as shown at length in *The Principles of Sociology*, in a chapter on "The Militant Type," that graduated subordination which we see in an army, characterizes a militant society at large more and more as militancy increases.

System, regulation, uniformity, compulsion—these words are being made familiar in discussions on social questions. Everywhere has arisen an unquestioned assumption that all things should be arranged after a definite plan. The recent course of public opinion shows how powerless, when opposed to prejudices and fancies, are those large truths which science discloses. One might have thought that in these days when it has been proved that the progress

189

of all life has been made possible only by unceasing variations, and that uniformity implies quiescence ending in death—one might have thought that the tendency would be, if not to foster variety, at any rate to give full opportunity for it. Yet a reverse tendency has been produced by the causes explained.

Though we have not reached a state like that boasted of by a French minister who said—" Now all the children in France are saying the same lesson," yet if we compare our present state with our state before board-schools were set up, we see a movement towards a like ideal. We have a " Code " to which managers and teachers must conform; and we have inspectors who see that the conceptions of the central authority are carried out. So far along some lines has the regimental system gone, that the Board of Education has had power to direct the metric system to be taught: over-taxed children are, at the will of the commanding officer, made to learn sets of measures which are not in use. Moreover, out of the elementary course there has developed a secondary course; and now have come technical schools to give boys knowledge and aptitude fitting them for various businesses. Schools of science, art-schools, and schools of design, too, have been set up; so that the State now prepares its pupils not for life in general only, but also for special careers. Meanwhile, as I prophesied thirty years ago would happen, the step has been taken from rearing the mind to rearing the body. In pursuance of the dogma that it is the duty of the community towards the child " to see that it has a proper chance as regards its equipment in life," it is held that food must be provided for hungry children; and there have been proposals to give shoes if parents fail to supply them. When it is added that there are over 30,000 children in industrial and truant schools, maintained and officered by the State, we see that even in a single generation great strides have been taken towards a regimental organization for moulding children after an approved pattern.

Having been prepared for life by government, citizens must have their activities controlled by law. The late Mr. Pleydell-Bouverie found that in Elizabeth's reign, out of 269 Acts, 68 were for regulating trade; and under James the First 33 out of 167 were similarly directed. These, all found useless or mischievous, have been repealed. But now, along with resuscitation of an older social type, there is a recurrence of old leanings towards the State-overseeing of industry. The restriction of child-labour in factories opened the way for regulations protecting more and more numerous classes of workers. Though the loss suffered by a mine-owner from an explosion is a stronger deterrent from risks than anything else, yet it is thought that precautions against explosions, can be insured only by inspectors: a belief which survives frequent explosions. The State, which has many accidents to its own vessels and often loses them, undertakes to protect men in the merchant service through a body of officials; though judging from the number of shipwrecks the effect is not manifest.

But let us turn from these scattered examples to examples of more general kinds. During the first part of the nineteenth century, while yet municipal governments were undeveloped, the activities of each were limited to a few all-essential matters—the maintenance of order by a small staff of constables, the paving and cleaning of the streets, the lighting of them by oil lamps, the making and maintaining of sewers. To meet the growing demands for conveniences of one or other kind, speculative citizens united their means and risked large sums in the hope that while subserving public wants they might gain rather than lose. Gas-companies arose early in the century; and from them the town authorities bought gas for lighting the streets. Presently came water-companies which on reservoirs, conduits, and distributing pipes, spent large sums. Thus town after town was greatly advantaged in pursuance of ordinary trade principles.* But in place of these private combina-

---

* When reading socialist and collectivist writers, who ignore the evils which towns-people once suffered, and vilify men who, while seeking profits, achieved these great benefits for others, I

tions of men, investing their savings and looking for interest, as men at large do, we now have municipal organizations which are usurping these businesses one after another and entering upon more. By the courtesy of the Town-Clerk of Birmingham I have obtained details of the various administrations in that city. We may begin with the all-essential one—the police force, which contains 800 men of seven grades. Next comes the public-works department, having eight divisions (including streets, trams, sewers and lighting), employing 1,726 men of fourteen denominations. In the water-supply administration we find 469 officials bearing twenty-five different names, besides other officials in the new Elan works. In the gas-department, there are 2,845 employés divided into seven classes; and then comes the more recent electric supply system with 113 men of four grades. After these may be named the fire-brigade with 72 men in five grades. The baths and parks divisions here follow with their 137 employés of eleven kinds.

---

have sometimes thought I should like to thrust them all back into " the good old times "—times before decent roads had been made by turnpike trusts; times when in London water from wells and conduits was eked out by water carried in leathern sacks over the backs of horses; times when for lighting the streets people had to hang candles (? lanterns) out of their windows, and when, even much later, pleasure-seekers were shown their ways home at night by link-boys carrying torches. Six months' experience of the miseries borne might change their feelings towards the companies they now speak of as public enemies.

Then we have the department of markets and fairs
employing 45 men of six kinds, and that of weights
and measures employing 13 men of four kinds.
There are three groups under the Health Committee,
entitled " interception," " sanitary," and " hospitals,"
of which the first has 585 men of four grades in its
pay, the next 75 men of five grades, and the last
178 men and women of five grades. The several
subdivisions of the estates administration (of which
one concerns the law-courts) employ 109 people variously distinguished. Following these may be set
down the City-asylum and the lunatic-asylum, of
which the one has 133 employés of eleven kinds and
the other 111 employés of sixteen kinds. After the
industrial school, which occupies 18 variously named
officials, come the school of art with its branches,
occupying 157, and the technical school occupying
66: in each case variously classed. Last come the
museum and the art-gallery employing 29 bearing
various titles. Over all these preside the officials of
the governing body, the town-clerk's department and
the treasurer's department, the one with 15 and the
other with 25 members of several grades. The entire
organization includes 7,800, very soon to exceed
8,000. Thus while there has been a replacing of
joint-stock companies by municipal administrations,
there have been developing many other administrations, undertaking other works. Each of these is,

as we see, like a military administration in having ranks subordinate one to another; and the aggregate of them reminds us of a series of companies united into regiments and brigades under a central command.

To Mr. William McBain who is familiar with the municipal government of Glasgow, and at the meeting of the British Association held there last year read a paper on the subject, I am indebted for the following brief account of the public organization of that city. The names of the divisions and their numbers run thus:—Headquarters, 60; police force, 1,400; works-department (to which belongs the supervision of new and existing buildings, streets and drains), 600; lighting-department, 700; cleansing-department, 600; city engineer and architect's department, 12; tramways, 3,500; water-supply, 527; gas, 3,000; electricity, 1,200; telephones, 400; fire-brigade, 121; public parks, galleries, museums and housing department, 300; baths and washing houses, —; markets, bazaars, halls, and blocks, 150; city assessor's department, 40; health department, 700; libraries, 100; labour bureau, 3; churches, —; total, 13,413. In addition to the municipal administrations there are in both cases school-board authorities and parochial authorities with their staffs: the number of graded officials and employés under their control in Glasgow being 4,000.

As intimated above, regimentation is another aspect of that general retrogression shown in growing imperialism and accompanying re-barbarization. Curious evidence of the way in which the one, like the other two, is carrying us back to mediævalism, is furnished by the town-records of Beverley recently published. The various businesses were of course, after the general usage of the time, carried on by members of gilds, which, including certain minor ones, numbered at the end of the fifteenth century, twenty-three. These groups of merchants, traders, and artisans, down even to porters, severally had a warden or alderman with two assistants or stewards and with two searchers or inspectors; while the component master-traders or burgesses had journeymen and apprentices. These organized bodies were under the control of a town-government, originally the Twelve Keepers, elected by the burgesses or masters, and these, while carrying on civic business, exercised authority over the gild-members, inflicting fines for various offences and breaches of rules. That is to say, though having different ends, these bodies were analogous to our modern administrations in respect of their graduated structure, their subjection to municipal government, and their inspection by its officers.

Not content with undertaking such businesses as those of joint-stock companies, our public agencies, general and local, are beginning to enter upon retail trading. We have not yet gone so far as the French, who have made the sale, as well as the manufacture, of tobacco and matches and gunpowder into State-monopolies, and who have State-establishments for the making of fine porcelain and tapestries, but we are taking steps in the same direction. Most conspicuous is municipal house-building. Over fifty years ago, and again in 1884, I pointed out that such enterprise is self-defeating, and recently Lord Avebury and Lord Rosebery have insisted on the same truth. But the public are now set upon it, and can no more be stopped by arguments and facts than a runaway horse can be stopped by pulling the reins. Other trades are being entered upon. The Liverpool Corporation sells sterilized milk for infants; and, arguing that it is proper to guard adults as well as infants from typhoid and tuberculosis, this sale of milk may be made general. The Corporation of Tunbridge Wells is carrying on the business of hop-growing—successfully, the town-clerk says; and it has set up a telephone system. At Torquay municipal farming has gone to the extent of making a profit from rabbits on its 2,200 acres of land, and feeding sheep instead of letting the grass to outsiders. Each step renders subsequent steps easier. Some three years or more ago a deputation to the London County Council advocated a system of municipal bakeries;

and there are signs that we may presently have in-
toxicating liquors sold by public agency: the Gothen-
burg system and the vodka-monopoly in Russia fur-
nishing precedents. When Collectivism has strengthened itself enough, there may come municipal gro-
ceries, and so on with other trades, until at length
manufacturers and distributors are formed into multitudinous departments, each with its head and its
ranks of subordinates and workers—regiments and
brigades. In France, beyond the fighting army, the
army of civil servants, ever increasing, has reached
nearly 900,000, and when all our businesses have
been municipalized, a larger number will have been
reached here.

Meanwhile the same process is going on among
artisans and others united into trade-unions. Made
somewhat different from one another by adjustments
to different occupations, they nevertheless show community in the division of their members into various
ranks—master-workmen, labourers, apprentices. As
of old in the gilds, there is a narrow limit to appren-
ticeships, and there are barriers against the rising
of workers of a lower rank into those of a higher.
There are rigid rules, and spies to detect breaches
of them. There are governing committees before
which transgressing members are called, and by which
heavy penalties for disobedience are imposed. Beyond these there are the penalties of expulsion and

consequent persecution when seeking employment. The local groups in each trade are subject to a central body partially controlling them; and there have been attempts to unite all the trades. So that the general principles of regimentation are displayed throughout. The whole organization is regarded as the workers' army; and the assertion has been made that in the conflict with masters the usages of war are justifiable.

Lastly let us note that this regimentation, now conspicuous in private organizations as in public ones, illustrates the concomitance between exercise of coercion and submission to coercion. The men who, pursuing what they think their trade-interests, trample on other men's freedom, surrender their own freedom while doing it. The members of a trade-union who assault non-unionists for offering to work on lower terms than themselves, thus denying their liberty of contract, have themselves yielded up their liberty of contract to the majority of their fellows and its governing body. While relinquishing their own rights to make the best of their own powers, they prevent outsiders from exercising similar rights, and stigmatize as a " blackleg," that is, a swindler, the man who insists on making his own bargains. Nay, they do more. Their leaders have applauded the Boer Government because it " protected the strikers but refused police protection for 'blacklegs.'" Already these men have made themselves semi-slaves to their trade-combinations, and with the further progress of imperialism, re-barbarization, and regimentation, their semi-slavery will end in complete slavery—a state which they will fully deserve.

WEATHER FORECASTS.

" Ah, it's too bright to last! " is an exclamation not unfrequently heard on a fine morning. Ill-based as are many common beliefs about the weather, a few are well-based, and this is one of them: little as those who utter it understand why.

A specially fine morning is nearly always the end of a fine night, that is, a night throughout all or most of which the sky has been free from clouds. During such a night the Earth's surface radiates its heat into space without impediment. There is no canopy of opaque vapour floating above, which radiates back to the Earth much of the heat which it receives from it. Hence, during the early part of the following day, before the sun is high, a low temperature is reached, alike by the exposed parts of the ground and by parts clothed with vegetation, as is shown by the large deposits of dew. The chilled surface is now a good condenser, and if the air is well charged with water, as commonly it is when the wind is westerly, and especially southwesterly, precipitation results: clouds begin to form and presently there

14

comes rain. If the air is not much charged with
water, as when it comes from the east, north-east, or
north, the probability of rain is much less; but there
may not unlikely ensue a cloudy day. By way of
impressing this relation of facts I have sometimes
expressed it facetiously thus:—When the Earth
throws off its blanket at night it takes cold and cries
in the morning.

Thus much by way of introduction. Let me pass
now to the larger topic on which I would dilate—the
relation between the kind of weather and the temperature of the Earth's surface, as illustrated in some
cases permanently and in other cases temporarily.

Permanent illustrations we have first of all in
the desert of Sahara and like rainless regions, where
the temperature of the surface is so high that precipitation is prevented: the radiant heat dissipating
all arriving clouds. A vicious circle is established.
Clouds cannot exist over the hot sand, and in the absence of rain and subsequent evaporation the sand
cannot be cooled. A converse relation of phenomena
is seen in mountainous regions. Having above them
smaller depths of air, elevated surfaces are colder
than the surfaces of valleys, and, being colder, bring
down water more readily. By storms, and by subsequent evaporation, they are continually chilled, and
therefore tend to condense more rain, or, as in Alpine
regions, snow. Here we have a vicious circle of the

opposite kind: from coldness of the surface come frequent precipitations, and these maintain the coldness of the surface.

That which holds permanently in these extreme cases must hold temporarily in less extreme cases— cases in which the surface, made in one way or other colder or warmer than usual, produces a greater or less tendency to rain than usual: a cause of rain which co-operates with other causes or conflicts with them. For the last twenty years I have occasionally noted this connexion of facts, and have several times discussed it with a friend who is, or was, concerned with the predictions of the Meteorological Office. In pursuance of our discussions I wrote to him from Dorking on July 20, 1888, a letter from which the following is an extract:—

Certainly two years ago—it may be three—I drew your attention to the temperature of the Earth as extending to a certain depth below the surface, as a factor in meteorology: arguing that when this superficial layer is colder than usual, it is a more efficient condenser and conduces to rainy weather.

You did not think anything of the suggestion, but I now draw your attention to our recent weather in illustration of my belief. The long cold spring, continuing on into summer, has so chilled the surface of the country that now, no matter what way the wind, cloud condenses every day and rain comes: there having been established, as in all such cases, a vicious circle—cold surface produces cloud, cloud prevents the warming of the surface; and when a certain stage has been reached there is no remedy save from some larger cycle of changes initiated elsewhere.

Then on March 8 of the next year, 1889, I wrote again as follows:—

When, on Wednesday morning, the wind changed according to forecast to S. and S.W., I made the remark—"Now we shall most likely have a great deal of rain, as the southerly and south-westerly winds will have to pass over a surface which has been chilled by a fortnight of frost and snow."

Some hours afterwards there came the evening paper of Wednesday in which there was the following forecast for the next day up to mid-day:—

[the extract was sent and is missing].

So, again, the next morning the forecast was:—

[this extract too was sent].

Thus it appears that no rain was anticipated until mid-day on Thursday, and that after that time the amount of rain anticipated was but small.

Now the facts have been very much at variance with these anticipations. The rain commenced 12 hours before the time when it was anticipated, viz., in the middle of the night on Wednesday, and here it has rained incessantly for more than 30 hours.

Here, then, I take it is a case in which the forecasts are wrong in taking no account of the temperature of the surface over which the wind passes. Last summer, as I pointed out to you, exemplified the general and continued effect of a surface chilled to a considerable depth by the long-continued cold and rain of the spring; and this case exemplifies the special and probably temporary effect of a surface greatly chilled but probably to a small depth.

In your reply last autumn you implied that my belief was that the temperature of the surface was the chief factor. I never said any such thing and never dreamed any such thing. I never supposed that it was anything like a chief factor, but merely a'leged that it was *a* factor which should be taken into account, and that under some conditions it just serves to turn the balance.

Before these dates and since, I have noted various facts respecting cloud-formation which serve in sundry ways to verify the belief above expressed. During one of the many autumn visits spent with my friends at Ardtornish (a new house at the head of Loch Aline, to which they gave a name adopted for the adjacent Ardtornish Castle on the Sound of Mull) I one day observed from this point of view, looking along the two and a half miles of Loch Aline to the Sound, that over the line of the Sound the clouds were thin. Over the mountains of Mull on the one side and the highlands of Morven on the other, the clouds were dark, that is, thick; whereas over the water of the Sound separating the two, the canopy of cloud was relatively light: the fact being, I presume, that the water in the Sound radiated more heat than did the surfaces of the hills on either side.

A different kind of evidence occurred on another occasion. While we were yachting up the Sleat Sound there came into view the island of Rum with its three mountain peaks. The day was clear, but over each of these peaks, some two or three hundred feet it may be above it, there was a solitary cloud, The appearance was at once curious and instructive. Adjacency to the cold surface of each peak, which was radiating little heat into space, established the conditions leading to condensation of vapour from the warmer air which drifted over the spot. More remarkable in appearance than the common cases in which a cloud continues to envelope the top of a mountain notwithstanding a breeze apparently strong enough to blow it away, were these three cases in which a cloud was detached but remained seemingly stationary above. Evidently the explanation in such cases is that the cloud is not really stationary, but that while on the leeward side the portions continually drifted away are forthwith dissolved, on the windward side other portions are formed from the wind continually arriving.

Here, in the South of England, evidences of other kinds have from time to time struck me. I may name, first, two instances of effects the converse of that described in the above-quoted letter as occurring in 1888, when a cold wet spring was followed by a cold wet summer. One of these instances was, I think, in 1893, when a warm and very dry spring was followed by a summer of drought; and the other was this year (1901), when, though to a less marked degree, a like sequence happened: both of these cases tending to show the state which results when the superficial layer of the Earth becomes warmer than usual. While spending last summer (1900) at Bepton, under the western end of the South Downs, I observed several examples of the influence which the high lands behind had upon the formation of cloud. On one occasion, at some height above the tops of the Downs, there extended as far as the eye could reach a canopy of cloud of the nimbus type. This canopy spread some distance towards the north, while further to the north there was a summer sky. This year (1901) at Petworth I observed a converse phenomenon. The weather was very hot, but over the comparatively cool surfaces of Blackdown and Hind Head some fleecy clouds had been formed. Drifting southwards these presently came over the valley of the Rother and then gradually dissolved: being dissipated by the radiated heat.

But the most striking support of my belief I have observed in the space between Brighton and Portslade. From the beach a level tract extends inland. On each occasion there was fine weather to seaward —a summer sky with a few drifting clouds, wafted by a gentle south-west breeze. The air remained clear for some distance inland from the shore, but at half a mile off or thereabouts there began to condense, at a hundred or more feet above the surface, a thin veil of cloud. This, being continually drifted away, thickened as it passed on, while a new portion of the thin veil was formed in its place, until, on looking landwards, one saw that a mile or two to the north a cloud-canopy covered the country. Two facts were here conspicuous. The first was that the air was made to condense its contained water by passing over a surface colder than that which it had previ-

ously been passing over. The second was that under conditions like those exemplified, a very slight
difference of surface-temperature might presently
produce a large effect by shutting out the source of
heat. Clearly, if the inland tract described had been
a little warmer, and had not caused the condensation
which formed a cloud-canopy, the country to the
north, remaining exposed to the sun, would have had
no tendency to form cloud and precipitate rain;
whereas the canopy of cloud, by intercepting the
sun's rays and keeping the surface relatively cold,
made more probable the continuance of cloudy and
rainy weather. When forces are nearly balanced the
addition of a small amount to one or the other may
cause a great and continued change.

It seems to me that we have here " a true cause "
of variations in weather. The only question is to
what extent it qualifies the effects of larger causes.
It is undeniable that the permanently dry regions and
the permanently wet regions exhibit the relation alleged, and it can hardly be denied that between these
extreme cases there must be multitudinous gradations of cases in which minor effects are produced.
Whether this factor can be so taken into account
as appreciably to affect forecasts may be doubted.
It has occurred to me, however, that if stations were
distributed with adequate frequency over the kingdom, each of which, duly fenced while duly exposed,

contained thermometers the bulbs of which were inserted in the ground to several depths, say three, six,
nine, and twelve inches, or more, it would be possible, by comparing the records of temperatures extending over years and over months, to judge whether
there would be an increased or a decreased tendency
to the rainy weather, or the fine weather, mainly
brought about by other causes. But I throw this out
merely as a suggestion.

THE REGRESSIVE MULTIPLICATION
OF CAUSES.

An ancestral tree is a familiar object—familiar because the desire to trace descent from some noteworthy person often prompts delineation of it. But no one draws up a converse ancestral tree—a tree representing all the ancestors of each preceding generation, multiplying as they recede: the four grandparents, the eight great-grandparents, the sixteen great-great-grandparents, the thirty-two, &c.; nearly all of them commonplace or obscure persons, descent from whom confers no distinction. Habitually ignoring the fact though he does, everyone is aware that of those men and women who form his own converse ancestral tree, branching and re-branching as it goes back in time, each gave a part of the constitution now possessed by him—each was a cause of multitudinous traits, most of them hidden, some unobtrusive, and a few conspicuous, as atavism occasionally proves. Though equality of influence cannot be alleged of all the members composing each receding generation, yet the exercise of *some* influence is undeniable. No one's nature would be the same were the share taken in forming it by any ancestor replaced by some other; and as the number of ancestors in each receding generation becomes greater, checked only by increasing coalescence of lines of ancestry, we see that the regressive multiplication of causes is exemplified in each person.

On looking into the matter more closely, we may observe that each of these causes was itself a complex cause, not only in the sense that each ancestor was an involved aggregate of structures and functions, but in the sense that each became a cause only by the aid of numerous co-operative causes—incidents, conditions, or antecedents, we must call them; since they were not themselves operative forces, but by their presence or absence allowed certain other forces to operate. If a certain ancestor and ancestress had been of different creeds; if one or both had had no property; if the lady had not recovered from small-pox without bearing marks; if illness had prevented one of them from attending a certain social gathering, or the other had been called away by business; or if some more attractive man had not been absent; and so on, and so on; the courtship would not have been initiated, the marriage would not have taken place, and there would not have been the child through whom the descent is traced. Moreover it is obvious that each of these co-operative antecedents itself depended on various other antecedents; so that, taking into account the innumerable causes implied by the innumerable marriages, there were practically infinite numbers of antecedents, every one of which exercised an influence over the result as seen in the now-existing descendant.

I have taken first this regressive multiplication of causes exhibited in the organic world, as being easy to follow. I pass now to the multitudinous cases, less easy to follow, exhibited by the inorganic world; for, commonly ignoring the fact though we do, each inorganic cause has an ancestry of inorganic causes, similarly multiplying as it recedes in time. This sandy beach bounded above by a bank of stones, affords good illustrations. A rill of water draining out of the shingle bank, runs over the sand, cutting a serpentine course, here shallow and outspread and there undercutting one side of its narrower channel. A pebble lying above the undermined side has fallen in. Look a little higher up, and you see that this minute streamlet has been deflected towards the undermined side by a large irregular boulder, the shape of which determined the course of the water. If you inquire for their antecedents you see that the irregularities of the boulder, due first to its heterogeneous composition, imply an infinity of processes that went on in geologic times, and also recall those actions of the breakers which have since rounded its prominent parts. Pursuing back a further line of causation you are shown that this boulder rolled down to its present place from the top edge of the shingle-bank, where it had been landed by a breaker at the last tide; and you are introduced to the countless causes which brought that boulder to the needful preceding place and to the forces which shaped the breaker that lodged it in its position: in both cases innumerable energies co-operating. Yet another retrogression brings you to that vibration produced in the adjacent road by a passing waggon, which shook the boulder from its place; then you have the complex group of antecedents implied by passage of the waggon; and so on perpetually. Thus is it with each of the apparently simple causes we see in operation. Always it is a composite cause; and each of the causes composing it is a composite cause. Shooting over a ledge of rock a small waterfall exhibits a force which seems one and homogeneous—a cause of change which we think of as simple. But if we trace back the stream we find that in it are united numerous streamlets, each of which is formed of many rills that severally drain away the water from surrounding herbage, and also convey the products of springs. A further recession brings us to the storms and the showers occurring at intervals, each presenting innumerable gravitating rain-drops. These, again, descend from clouds which have been drifting and eddying on their way from the Atlantic seaboard; and a thousand or more miles off the molecules forming these clouds were evaporated from ocean-surfaces too wide and various to conceive. So that the forces exercised by the mass of molecules in the waterfall have had antecedents branching and re-branching to an unimaginable degree as they are traced back.

When studying the cosmic process we are prone to look in advance. We watch the changes now taking place and think of those which will presently take place. When contemplating a force tacitly assumed to be simple, we observe how, falling on any aggregate, the effects it produces are perpetually multiplied, how there go on corresponding differentiations of structure, while the original force and its derived forces are themselves differentiated; and we observe how, under certain conditions, there go on integrations of structure and corresponding integrations of forces. But rightly to conceive the cosmic process we must give equal attention to the fact that throughout the past there have been perpetual differentiations of matters and of forces, and that under some conditions there have been perpetual integrations of matters and of forces: the result being that the factors of the cosmic process immediately within our ken, have histories in the past approximately as complex as are the histories which will result from them in the future. Continually in our analyses and syntheses we begin with Here and Now; whereas in the

totality of things there is no Here and no Now, but
only a momentary aspect of a transformation which,
though in the course of immeasurable time becoming
more involved, is approximately as involved in the
immediate past as it will be in the immediate future
—in the totality of things I say, because in things
taken separately it is otherwise. Hence we have to
regard each cause we see in operation as resulting
from an integration of causes, or rather of forces,
conditions, antecedents, becoming more complex with
each step of retrogression, carrying us back to an
infinite complexity.

To many readers it will be manifest that the foregoing paragraphs, duly elaborated, should have
formed a chapter in *First Principles*. More than a
year ago I issued the sixth edition of that work, re-
vised up to date: conceiving it then, as I conceive it
now, to be the final edition; for it is not likely that
the whole of it will be sold before my death. Thus
no opportunity is likely to occur for incorporating
what I have recently discovered should have been
set forth as part of the general doctrine contained
in that work; and I have therefore no alternative
but to include a brief exposition of it in this miscellaneous volume.

SANITATION IN THEORY AND PRACTICE.

AFTER lying unused for nearly fifty years, an almost forgotten incident will serve to introduce some comments on the doings of our guardians of the public health. It occurred at a little dinner given by a friend, long since deceased without leaving descendants, Mr. F. O. Ward, active in the sanitary agitation then carried on, and, I believe, a writer of occasional leaders on water-supply and other such matters in *The Times*. He was an enthusiast and soon found occasion to bring up his favourite topic. The form his talk took was an unstinted laudation of his friend Edwin Chadwick, the leader of the movement; and the particular trait singled out for praise was his perseverance in carrying out vast investigations. One illustration given was that if he needed proof of some point in his case, he instructed a man to examine and report, and if the man did not bring back the evidence he desired, he sent him about his business and dispatched another; meting out like measure to him too, if he failed to furnish statements of the required kind; and so on, and so on,

216

until he got the proof he wanted. All this was said with apparent unconsciousness of the damaging implications respecting Blue Books—the disclosure of the way in which a strong case is made out by omitting facts which do not support the foregone conclusion. Twice since that time I have had occasion to look into these masses of officially-collected evidence, and in both cases have seen how the bias of those concerned has vitiated the conclusions drawn.

Among those now living few remember how, in the early fifties there was widely disseminated the idea, naturally arising and readily accepted, that fevers of one or other kind are produced by noisome odours—stinks and stenches. What proposition seemed more reasonable than that the repulsive smells arising from decomposing matter carried with them the germs of diseases, or else that the smells themselves were the causes of diseases? Slums and their surroundings, where epidemics arose, were commonly characterized by malodours proceeding from dirt, from refuse-heaps, and from obstructed drains. Was not the explanation obvious? After the usual style of reasoning, which proceeds by the method of agreement unchecked by the method of difference, it was concluded that as these two things habitually went together, the one was the cause of the other. It was not asked whether these places where disease was rife were not also places inhabited

15

by people leading unhealthy lives—drunkards, prostitutes, beggars, and half-starved men and women, who were, in consequence of their modes of life, their bad feeding and over-crowding, on the highway to death. It was not asked whether the diseases were not due to these causes rather than to the smells. The verdicts of the nostrils were willingly assumed to be verified by statistics.

And yet the counter-evidence was overwhelming. In every village throughout the kingdom, each of the half-dozen farms, by its yard full of manure, by its cow-sheds, and by its stables, severally reeking with the gases from decomposing matter, furnished a contradiction to the belief that ordinary unpleasant odours are pernicious. Places which, according to current sanitary doctrines, ought to be centres of disease, prove to be quite healthful—so healthful, indeed, that invalids frequently take lodgings in farm-houses where they are exposed to these products of decaying excreta. Nor need we go to the country for disproofs. They are supplied by all the stables in great towns—stables in which grooms, ostlers, and others, spend great parts of their lives, and over which in many cases families reside. Nay, London affords a still more conspicuous contradiction. Throughout the hottest months of the year the horse-dung scattered over the streets is perpetually ground down by carriage wheels, occasionally sprinkled by water-carts, and shone on by the July or August sun: the disgusting odour emitted in hot weather yielding ample proof of the decomposition taking place in every thoroughfare. What is the result? None, so far as the Bills of Mortality tell us. The deaths per thousand are not higher in number at that time than at other times, and are, indeed, occasionally lower than at this salubrious place, Brighton. Once more, personal observation has supplied me with a yet more striking disproof of the notion that was established by garbled evidence in past years. Visits frequently paid in the autumn to certain delightful friends, who at that season migrate from London to their estate on the western coast of Scotland, repeatedly obliged me to go by steamer down the Clyde, sometimes in July sometimes in August; and on more occasions than one I have been compelled, during part of the passage between Glasgow and Greenock, to hold my handkerchief to my nose so as to minimize my perception of the abominable smell given off from the drainage of Glasgow poured into the river. Now all along its banks are ship-yards where thousands of men saw and hammer all day long, and had this stench been the fever-breeding agent which we are led to suppose, these men ought to have been swept away wholesale. Yet there were no statements of unusual mortality among them.

But now, accepting for a moment these doctrines which we have been industriously taught, let us see what have been the measures taken in pursuance of them. It was found that ordinary soil is a good disinfectant, and that effete matters mixed with it, while having their disagreeable odours destroyed, increase its fertility. What was the inference? Evidently that if sewage was properly distributed over areas of land, it would lose that disease-producing quality associated with its noisomeness, at the same time that the crops would be increased. Sewage farms resulted from this inference. It was forgotten that the disinfecting power of soil is dependent on its ability to absorb the matters mixed with it or poured over it, and that as soon as it becomes saturated it loses its disinfecting power. This conclusion, obvious one would have thought even to the uninstructed, was not drawn by those in authority. The result was that the irrigated lands became widespread sources of these gases we have been taught to dread. Along with cases of which I have read, one case has come under my personal notice. Friends of mine living some four miles from a sewage farm, were so much annoyed by the repulsive odours frequently wafted from it, that they had thoughts of leaving their house. Of course the nuisance suffered by them was suffered still more by hosts of people in nearer places, according as the wind brought the foul gas over them or carried it elsewhere. And this wide diffusion of noisome effluvia, said in other cases to be productive of disease, went on until the town of Burton had to spend a large sum in partially deodorizing the sewage before distributing it.

But now observe what have simultaneously been the measures taken in towns to exclude the mischiefs ascribed to foul gases. The ventilation of sewers has been insisted upon as a needful prophylactic, and nowadays one sees galvanized iron pipes, disfiguring the sides of buildings, arranged for carrying away those products of decomposition which, by the sewage-farms, are spread abroad for people to breathe. That which, in small quantity, is injurious in the one place is, in large quantity, innocuous in the other! Nay, this is not all. Where alterations in the drainage of houses are made, and where, by consequence, certain old drains are cut off as useless, it is common to require that these shall be destroyed. Though very shortly there will be nothing left in them to decompose, and though, during the interval, any escaping gas must pass through six, eight, or more feet of that soil said to be so effective as a disinfectant, they must be made away with! Truly the ancient figure of straining at a gnat and swallowing a camel is utterly inadequate to express the folly of these proceedings.

How is it that beliefs so conspicuously fallacious have been established and are maintained by central and local authorities and their employés? There has developed a bureaucracy which has an interest in keeping up these delusions; and the members of which, individually, have interests in insisting upon these needless expenditures. Every organized body of men tends to grow, and tends to magnify its own importance. For the last half-century the military class has been raising an outcry about our defence-lessness, notwithstanding successive additions to the army. Continually there have been urgent demands from admirals and captains that our navy shall be increased; and when it has been increased there have been demands for further increases. Similarly with the State-Church. Under the plea of "spiritual destitution" the erection of more churches has been urged by unbeneficed clergy, and then incomes for incumbents have been asked. And under kindred influences the sanitary class, which has grown up since Chadwick's day, ever exaggerates the evils to be dealt with while tacitly exalting its own members. A surveyor employed by a public body has to prove himself a vigilant man, and he does this by finding fault wherever there is a possible occasion—has, in fact, no other way of getting a reputation. So, too, if an in-coming tenant engages a surveyor, he chooses one recommended as experienced and careful, and one having this character has obtained it by exaggerating defects and insisting on needless changes. A man who frequently reports that nothing needs doing is looked at sceptically, as a doctor is looked at when he prescribes no medicine.

Yet another cause co-operates. New sanitary appliances are continually being devised, sanctioned by authority, and required by surveyors; and surveyors may have, and certainly sometimes do have, personal interests in pushing the use of them: either as being shareholders in the companies they are manufactured by, or as receiving percentages on the numbers sold through their recommendation. In these days when illegitimate commissions are being disclosed, it is folly to suppose that here, where there is an obvious method of obtaining secret profits, it will not be used.

"But what does it matter?" will be exclaimed by some random readers. "It simply entails extra costs on landlords or on classes of tenants who can well bear them." Here is a sample of those vicious ways of thinking common in social affairs. As far back as 1850 I pointed out the evils entailed by artificially raising the costs of houses, and since then (see *The Man* versus *The State*, pp. 51–5) I have given definite proof that the multiplication of sanitary requirements often arrests the building of small houses.

And then comes a further mischief. As a sequence of this law-made deficiency of house-accommodation, there has been growing louder a complaint about the " houseless poor," with frequent newspaper articles on " The Housing Problem "; tacitly assuming that it is a public business to supply people with fit abodes. For equally valid reasons there may by-and-by be agitated the " food problem," and then the " clothing problem "; whereupon socialism will be achieved.

GYMNASTICS.

Some year or two ago, in *Harper's Magazine* (unfortunately I did not note the date) I read the judgment of an expert which confirmed that ill-opinion of gymnastics I have long entertained. It was contained in an essay entitled "Non-Hygienic Gymnastics," by Mr. Richard Buckham, who quoted as follows from "a well-known teacher of physical development" in New York:—

"I have no hesitation in saying that our systems of athletic training, at least the most of those now in vogue, are not only vicious in principle, but tend to break down the system, shorten life, and generally do more harm than good. I have made a study of the subject for many years, and I long ago began to inquire why it is that so-called athletes usually die young, or are not nearly so vigorous at forty-five or fifty as the man who has rigorously neglected any sort of training, and perhaps even exercise. That such is the fact there is no room for doubt. Athletes do die young. I do not mean by all this that I do not regard athletic sport of various kinds as healthy and valuable. On the contrary, I do, just as long as they are pleasurable, and are play and not work. But when your young athlete begins to train for a rowing contest or for the football team, or for anything like that, he is going to an excess, and that is just as bad as excess in any other way—in business, in mental labor, or in anything else. And the chances are that he will exhaust his system, come out with a weak heart or some other trouble, and be physically damaged for the remainder of his life. What the man of to-day needs most is not athletics in a gymnasium, but plenty of fresh air in his lungs. Instead of a quantity of violent exercise that leaves him weak for several hours afterward, he needs to learn to breathe right, stand right, and sit right."

Belief in the virtues of gymnastics, widespread and indeed almost universal, embodies several grave errors. The first to be here commented upon is the identification of muscular strength with constitutional strength. It is assumed that one who can lift great weights, jump great heights, or run great distances, is proved by these abilities to be fitted for withstanding the strains of life—doing hard work, bearing unfavourable conditions, and so on. The inference is erroneous. Darwin described the dwarfish Fuegians as being so degraded in appearance as scarcely to look like human beings; and yet he tells us that they could with impunity let the snow fall and melt upon their naked skins. A disturbance of the constitutional balance which would be fatal to a European was to them innocuous. Similarly with animals. It is recognized by breeders that the small unimproved French breeds are more hardy than the large improved English breeds. Muscularity and the putting out of great mechanical force, are no measures of strength in that sense of the word which chiefly concerns men. Such power of limb as results from the daily activities of boyhood—say the ability, even in early youth, to walk

more than forty miles in a day (I speak from personal experience)—is quite enough in preparation
for the contingencies of ordinary life, and of life
deviating a good deal from the ordinary.

Not only is there error in assuming that increase
of muscular power and increase of general vigour
necessarily go together, but there is error in assuming that the reverse connexion cannot hold. It is
taken for granted that general vigour, if not increased, is at any rate not decreased. But this is
untrue. There are obvious physiological reasons
for the injurious results testified to by the expert
quoted above. The current belief takes no account
of cost. It is supposed that certain sets of muscles
can be greatly developed without the system at large
being so taxed as to cause mischief. But when it is
remembered that the alimentary organs have but
a limited ability, and that the blood they furnish
has to serve for all purposes, it will be understood
that you cannot greatly develop certain large ex-
ternal parts without appreciably drawing upon the
supplies needed for repair and growth of other ex-
ternal parts, and also of those internal parts which
carry on the life; and that therefore the abnormal
powers acquired by gymnasts may be at the cost of
constitutional deterioration.

There has to be added the further great mistake
that it matters not whether exercise is pleasurable

or otherwise.   The current conception is that, given a certain amount of muscular activity gone through, the beneficial effect is the same if, instead of an accompanying gratification, there is an accompanying indifference, or even that partial pain which great strain implies.   Again we meet with a physiological blunder.   Every medical man has daily proof that an agreeable state of feeling goes a long way towards curing illness; and there is scarcely a household in which all members have not from time to time seen illustrations of this truth.   Yet there seems a refusal to draw the inference that if pleasure is beneficial to an invalid, so also is it to a person in health.   In him the effect is not conspicuous, but it is there.   As certain as it is that a country walk through fine scenery is more invigorating than an equal number of steps up and down a hall; so certain is it that the muscular activity of a game, accompanied by the ordinary exhilaration, invigorates more than the same amount of muscular activity in the shape of gymnastics.

Underneath these errors lies the vicious conception which pervades the thoughts of teachers at large.   Culture, no matter of what kind, must take the shape of tasks.   In the minds of most people education and pleasure are mutually exclusive ideas. Disagreeable strain is regarded as necessarily accompanying mental development; and we here see that the same connexion of thoughts is extended to bodily development: this must be achieved by the disagreeable muscular strains constituting gymnastics. Moreover, throughout we are shown the ingrained faith in coercion. Pupil and master are correlatives; and the master is conceived as one who exercises such force as he deems needful. Nowadays the coercive relation, once marked enough, is fading; but the dominant idea in the pupil's mind continues to be fulfilment of the master's will, rather than acquisition of knowledge and mental power. And if in the bodily culture known as gymnastics, the mastery of the instructor is no longer conspicuous (save in Germany), yet here also there survives the thought of fulfilling requirements and of subjection to the demands of the system.

Alike among early civilized races and among barbarians, war originated gymnastics; and the theory and practice of gymnastics have all along remained congruous with the militant type of society: witness the present state of Germany. The endurance of painful efforts and the disregard of pleasure, have had their appropriateness to social states in which bodily prowess was of chief importance; and a physical discipline, pushed even to the extent of an earlier break-up of the constitution, was not without a good political defence. But with the advance towards a peaceful state of society, the need for making strength of limb a chief qualification in the citizen diminishes, and along with its diminution, coercive and ascetic culture loses its fitness. In place of artificial appliances for bodily development come the natural appliances furnished by games and spontaneous exercises.

EUTHANASIA.

THROUGH many years, personal experiences have drawn my attention to the effect of attitude on the cerebral circulation, and something like a decade ago my thoughts passed from the effect of attitude to the effect of motion. It occurred to me that by centrifugal force the cerebral circulation might easily be regulated: now increase in the supply of blood to the brain being produced and now decrease. Supposing the patient to be placed with his head in the centre of a table capable of being made to revolve on its axis, a moderate speed of rotation would cause abstraction of blood from the head and determination of it towards the feet; while, contrariwise, if his feet were placed in the centre and his head at the circumference, his head would become congested. Of course I saw at once that such proceedings would be extremely dangerous. But it was manifest that by modified arrangements dangers might be avoided. If the patient were placed not radially but in a transverse position, then the relative distances of the head and feet from the centre might be so adjusted as to have any degree of inequality. In that case rotation would produce any desired amount of effect on the circulation through the brain.

My idea did not go beyond the stage of speculation, for it was obvious that the required appliances would be expensive and would require a large room to themselves, so that the experiment could not be tried in my own house. Presently I reverted to the idea in its first form—head in the centre and feet at the periphery; and it occurred to me that the fatal result quickly entailed on a patient so placed, even when the velocity of rotation was moderate, was a fatal result which might intentionally be produced where the death-penalty had been pronounced. Supposing the sentiment of revenge to be excluded, and supposing it decided that criminals of an extremely degraded type may best be put out of existence, there would thus be provided for them a simple means of euthanasia. The effects of rotation would be first faintness, and then insensibility—an insensibility soon made permanent if rotation was continued. For when, after a few revolutions at considerable speed, the brain had been emptied of blood, as well as the ascending aorta and in large measure the heart, cessation could not be followed by a back-flow from the lower parts of the body sufficient to re-establish the actions of the organs thus thrown out of gear; and, unquestionably, continuance of rotation for some time would make revival altogether impossible.

For a while I entertained the thought of having the experiment tried at the Home for Lost Dogs, where I believe that ownerless and worthless dogs are made away with by some anæsthetic. My scheme, as modified for this experiment, was not that of a rotating table, but that of two radially-placed wings on opposite sides of a vertical rotating axis; each being trough-shaped, the one to contain the victim and the other to contain such weights as balanced it, so as to prevent that irregularity of motion which arises when the masses of matter on opposite sides of an axis of rotation are not in equilibrium. But to seek out the drawing instruments of my engineering days, and make the requisite design and working drawings, and afterwards to superintend the artisans, threatened to be too serious a business. Suspension of more important work would have been needful, for I had no longer energy enough to carry on the two at once. Hence the idea dropped.

I name it here in the hope that some one with adequate time and means will do that which I was compelled to leave undone.

16

THE REFORM OF COMPANY–LAW.

So far as I have observed, projects for Company-law reform have concerned only the methods pursued in the formation of companies. They have had for their aims to restrain the fraudulent doings of promoters, and to prevent delusion of the public by the parading of apparently-responsible directors whose influential names have been indirectly purchased. But no thought appears to have been given to abuses existing in the administrations of established companies. Extremely grave evils are, however, to be observed in these, and it is high time they should be checked.

Bred of the great political superstition that there is no limit to the powers of a Parliamentary majority (except the limit of physical impossibility) there has long prevailed, and now appears more dominant than ever, the notion that, given any kind of elected body—council, directors, or what not—which was created for a generally-understood purpose, a majority of it may undertake other purposes never contemplated when its members were appointed. In an

article on " Railway Morals and Railway Policy,"
published in the *Edinburgh Review* for October,
1854 (see *Essays*, library edition, vol. III), I pointed
out the great mischiefs arising from this misinterpre-
tation of the proprietary contract, and gave an illustration of the way in which there arose an abnormal
forcing on of extensions and branch lines: directors
and all connected with the administration being enabled, by guaranteed shares, to make profits at the
expense of the shareholders at large. Since then this
practice of committing companies to subsidiary un-
dertakings, not originally even dreamed of, has greatly extended: hotels, docks, lines of steamers, mines,
&c., being successively forced on men who originally
subscribed money to make a railway from A to B.

And now we see the like illegitimate extension
taking place in industrial companies. Directors who
were elected simply to carry on the business of brew-
ing, are allowed to enter on speculative enterprises;
buying not ordinary tied-houses only, but great hotels, and even subscribing large sums to speculative
enterprises utterly alien to their own: witness the
case of Samuel Allsopp and Sons, Limited, as recently reported (*The Times*, August 31, 1901): the result being an enormous loss and a depreciation of
shares. Another example is furnished by the Linotype Company, formed originally for the purpose of
making and selling Linotype machines. By the ac-

tion of its directors this company has been led into making printing appliances of various kinds; so that those who joined in an enterprise of which they found reason to think well, are now committed to many other enterprises which they know nothing about. Of this abuse, taking another form, an extreme case is furnished by the doings of the London and Globe Finance Corporation, as shown in recent exposures. Here the board became simply a speculator to an enormous extent, buying up vast amounts of mining shares to obtain permanent control; and the various transactions, altogether unknown to the proprietary, were also in chief measure unknown to all the directors save one—the managing director. Besides such excesses of directorial power there are other excesses shown by committing the proprietors to large organic changes. At a recent meeting of the Metropolitan District Railway, the chairman pointed out that had it not been for the immense error committed by past boards of directors, in issuing perpetual Six per cent. debentures and perpetual Five per cent. preference stock, the company would now be a prosperous concern.

How directorial power should be curbed is a difficult question to answer. More deliberation might perhaps be insisted on. Measures of importance are too easily decided and carried out by boards of directors. Should there not be restraints akin to those

which our two legislative houses impose on themselves by requiring a second and a third consideration? That there exists, in some cases at least, as I
have ascertained, a course of business which involves
re-considerations is true; but something more systematic would probably be beneficial. It may also be
reasonably asked whether all measures implying considerable changes, or expenditures of large amounts,
should not be referred to the proprietary—whether
before a final decision there should not be something
like a *referendum*. Doubtless most of the proprietors would be incapable of judging, and in so far the
procedure would be inoperative; but from some
capable business-men would come judgments for and
against, with reasons which might weigh; and beyond that, there would, in important cases, be the
check put by publication in the financial Press; for
of course through one or other channel the information would pass from the proprietary to the public.
Is it not likely that when the directors of a brewery
company were obliged thus to let men at large know
that they were proposing to speculate in the shares of
an amusement company, the Press-criticisms would
check them, to the great advantage of the proprietary? And might not the unwisdom of the proposal
to saddle the shareholders of a railway-company with
a large amount of Five per cent. perpetual preference stock and perpetual Six per cent. debentures,

when commented upon by the railway-journals, suffice to prevent so impolitic a step? "But would not anything like a *referendum* be a great hindrance to business?" Hindrance? Yes; this is exactly the thing wanted. Within the last fifty years a hundred millions of capital have been lost from want of such hindrances.

Abuses which might readily have been foreseen have arisen from the practice of making the chairman of a board of directors also chairman of the meeting of proprietors—abuses which would not have existed had there been a practice like that which, in the House of Commons, results in a Speaker who is independent alike of the party in power and of the opposition. The present arrangement is conspicuously absurd. At a periodical gathering of shareholders the directors have to render an account of their stewardship, and to ask for the shareholders' approval of what they have done. Yet such being the purpose it is thought proper that the chief steward shall preside and regulate the proceedings! Of course as chairman he has large power of impeding opponents and aiding those who support the board. He may assert that a speech is out of order, or that it must be ended from lack of time, or that other business must be brought forward; or appointed mouth-pieces of the board in the meeting may interrupt or contradict; so that, save in cases of extreme misbehaviour arousing the general anger of the proprietary, there is little chance that an opposition will make itself fairly heard. But it needs no detail to show that if you give a board whose doings are to be examined, power over the proceedings of the examining body, that power will inevitably be used to hinder investigation and prevent blame.

That the current practice entails conspicuous mischiefs, here is a proof. Company A, with good prospects, needs more capital and has exhausted its means of obtaining it. As a last resort there is formed company B, consisting mainly of large shareholders in company A who have confidence in its future. An agreement is made under which company B is to buy all the products made by company A and pay cash for them; thus practically increasing company A's capital, by rendering needless the amount required for giving credit. But company B does this only on condition of receiving a large commission on the sale of company A's goods. At the same time company B enters upon a like commission-business in the sale of machines of other kinds. Now this arrangement under which, as said by its chairman, company B becomes practically a banker to company A, obtaining high interest on loans, is of limited duration—five years or ten years, I do not remember which. It is therefore company B's interest to obtain a renewal of the agreement, so as to force company A to go on selling machines through its agency and paying this high commission; though company A, having become highly prosperous, no longer needs any such banking aid. But now mark the significant fact that the same gentleman is chairman of both companies. As having a large investment in company B, which reaps immense dividends, he is, as shown by his utterances, strongly desirous of obtaining a renewal of the agreement. Hence when presiding over a meeting of company A he is swayed by interests at variance with those of its shareholders, and is prompted to get the agreement renewed by whatever means he can—say, among others, the postponement of the question of renewal till the close of the meeting, when a large number have gone away leaving behind those most interested in getting the renewal. Clearly under the presidency of one who was unconcerned in the result, company A would be much less likely to be disadvantaged.

What remedy is there for this defect in the present system of procedure? The appointment of a chairman on the spur of the moment would not answer; since, by following plans previously laid, the board would readily get its own nominee elected. Much as one may dislike invoking public agency, yet it may be argued that for the due administration of justice, it would be fit that there should be some ten

or more official chairmen to company-meetings, analogous to Official Referees, each of whom should receive the day before any meeting he was appointed
to by a public authority, the programme of business
to be gone through.

One more evil, greater even than those above described, remains. This is the system of voting by
proxy. As originally devised, a proxy was a means
of enabling one who could not attend a meeting, but
had reasons for voting with or against some proposal,
to register his vote by the agency of a person with
whom he was in agreement, or on whose judgment
he could rely. It was never intended to be a surrender of judgment on all and every matter into the
hands of some one, usually unknown, who might or
might not be an unbiassed judge. Into this, however, the system has grown. On receiving from the
secretary a form duly stamped and issued at the cost
of the company, and naming the chairman, or if not,
some alternative director, or if not, another director,
and so on, as his proxy, the ordinary unreflecting
shareholder, instead of throwing it into the fire or
waste-paper basket, thinks himself bound to sign it,
filled up in favour of one or other of those named—is
under a vague feeling of obligation that he must do
something with it in the manner suggested. If asked
his reason for thus giving to an unknown person

power to decide an unknown matter, he replies that the directors' interests are the same as his, and that they know more about the company's affairs than he does. As I have pointed out in the essay above named, and have there conclusively shown by facts, this supposed unity of interests often does not exist, and I have above further proved this: the interests of directors may be in sundry ways at variance with those of proprietors. Yet the effect of this proxy-system as now developed is to give directors uncontrolled powers. The shareholders who have unquestioning faith in the governing body are so numerous, that their votes overwhelm the votes of those who attend the meetings, and either already know a good deal about the matters to be decided or gain insight into them during the proceedings. In the hands of interested manipulators the ignorance of the many is used to extinguish the knowledge of the few. And then, naming the large number of proxies they have received, the directors tacitly boast of the confidence placed in them and the implied justification of their policy. The last and most striking illustration of this which I have observed, was furnished by a meeting of the London and Globe Finance Corporation, reported in *The Times* for January 10, 1901—a company the transactions of which had been, and were then, under grave suspicion. But the infatuated shareholders did not waver, as was shown by the

following statement of the managing director and
autocrat :—

"Mr. Whitaker Wright, in seconding the motion, stated
that the directors had received proxies for nearly 1,000,000
shares in the company (cheers); the proxies lodged in opposition amounted to 26,394 shares ; and proxies representing 4,987
shares had come in too late. That showed the view of the
shareholders."

The worth of this boasted confidence may be judged
by the fact that the company is now in course of
liquidation under an order of the Court.

But the proxy-system does more than enable directors to carry out schemes that are at variance with
the interest of proprietors: it also makes the board
an invulnerable oligarchy. In a case which I have
in mind (being a shareholder), the chairman trium-
phantly specified the great number of proxies in
their hands which they had used for the re-election
of a director whose place had, in the ordinary routine, been vacated. What corollary is to be drawn?
Spite of opposition, the board as a whole may, by the
use of proxies sent to its members, insure the re-election of any one of their number who is about to re-
tire. Or otherwise the chairman, in whose favour
the great mass of the proxies are made out, is enabled, when any member of the board becomes dis-
agreeably recalcitrant—a " guinea-pig " who unex-
pectedly proves to have a will of his own—to use his
proxies in favour of some new candidiate whom he

has picked out.   Thus the representative government
of a company is reduced to a farce.   The board becomes first an oligarchy and then an autocracy.

Do I hope for any results from these protests, or
any such protests?   No; there is a conclusive reason
why no changes of the kind required will be made.
Three out of four of our legislators have seats on one
or other board of directors: some of them seats on
many boards.   The reforms made by them in their
capacity of legislators would restrict their powers in
their capacity of directors.   Any one who expects
that they will thus sacrifice themselves takes a view
of human nature altogether at variance with experience.

SOME MUSICAL HERESIES.

It has been noted as curious that while Newton rejected the undulatory theory of light propounded by Huyghens, Huyghens refused to accept the theory of universal gravitation set forth by Newton.

Why do I name here this seemingly irrelevant fact? Simply as an illustration of the truth that the opinions of experts, even of supreme rank, are not always to be accepted as final. Doctrines rejected by the highest authorities sometimes prove true, and consequently some small scepticism concerning beliefs apparently unquestionable may be allowed. This must be my excuse for venturing opinions which will not meet with acceptance among experts in music.

And first let me note that musical experts are specially exposed to perverting influences. Music has two distinct components—the sensational and the relational. One part of the impression it produces results from the character of the tones, and the other part from the mode of combination of the tones. The feeling a piece of music produces may be in various degrees pleasurable or sometimes painful, ac-

cording as the component tones have *timbres* that
are in various degrees agreeable or sometimes even
disagreeable; while there is another pleasure which
the successions and combinations of tones may give
apart from their qualities. From this platitude
there is a corollary which here concerns us. The
tones are the products of the voices or instruments
employed, and though the singer and the player respectively try to improve them, they are in their
main qualities fixed. The chief part of the executive skill to be gained, especially by the instrumen-
talist, is skill in producing successions of tones in
the most perfect way, or, as on the piano, combinations of tones: the relational element of the music
predominates in his thoughts. Still more is this so
with the composer. In his mind the relational element is practically the exclusive element. While he
desires that his ideas shall be expressed in fine tones,
and tones appropriately varied, yet, as composer, he
is almost wholly occupied with such arrangements of
tones, successive and simultaneous, as will convey
his ideas. The very name composer implies this.
Hence it happens that in chief measure the composer,
and in large measure the performer, when judging
of a musical effect, thinks more of its relational characters than of its sensational characters. A Paga-
nini will take greater pride in his marvellous dexter-
ity of arm and finger than in the *timbres* of his tones,

though he desires that these also shall be good. And similarly a Beethoven, when listening to a symphony he has composed, will receive greater gratification from the beautiful successions and complexes of its notes, than from the tones of the various instruments, however good they may be. Hence, then, musicians of both classes necessarily tend to overvalue the relational elements. If the relational elements are good they will be apt to condone defects in the sensational elements: witness the way in which they tolerate the grunts made in playing a *forte* passage on the double bass.

Among sequences of the implied tendency, one is their exaltation of the violin and forgiveness of its grave defects. It is currently called a perfect instrument—perfect in the sense that it expresses with facility all the relational elements of music—all the varieties of contrasts and kinds of contrasts among tones. But the poorness of the tones themselves is overlooked. They have two incurable defects. One is conspicuous—the hiss of the bow and production of high over-tones as it is drawn over the string, which, however much subdued by a first-rate player, can never be wholly got rid of. The other, though not conspicuous, is no less great, perhaps even greater. The sounds come from strings restrained in their vibrations. Continuous contact of the bow prevents each string from reaching the normal limit of its swing in either direction, and the character of the air-waves produced differs from what it would be were the oscillations unchecked. There is clear proof of this. Contrast the tones of a violin with the tones of an Æolian harp. The two are alike in the respect that their vibrating strings are attached to sounding boxes, but unlike in the respect that the vibrations are in the one case checked and in the other case unchecked. No one will deny that the sounds of the Æolian harp are far sweeter than those of the violin: which last, indeed, suggest the voice of a shrew in a good temper.

To this contentment of musicians with an instrument so imperfect in its tones though perfect in its relational expressiveness, we may ascribe the characters of orchestras; since in them the tones of stringed instruments so greatly predominate. We are all of us, composers and musicians included, brought up in passive acceptance of ideas, sentiments, and usages, political, religious, and social, and I may here add artistic. We accept the qualities of orchestral music as in a sense necessary; never asking whether they are or are not all that can be desired. But if we succeed in escaping from these influences of custom, we may perceive that orchestras are very defective. Beauty they can render; grace they can render; delicacy they can render; but where is the dignity, where is the grandeur? There is a lack of

adequate impressiveness. Think of the volume and
quality of the tones coming from an organ, and then
think of those coming from an orchestra. There is
a massive emotion produced by the one which the
other never produces: you cannot get dignity from a
number of violins. This under-valuation of the sensational element in music is, I think, clearly shown
by the way in which musicians tolerate the performance of chamber-music in a great hall. For many
years past, the Monday Popular Concerts and the
Saturday-afternoon Rehearsals, have made this abuse
conspicuous. I say advisedly—abuse, for it is utterly at variance with the intentions of the composers.
A quartet or a piece for five or six stringed instruments, is intended to be played in a small room: the
composer knowing that only by the reverberation it
gives can there be produced that volume of sound required for the harmonies; since, necessarily, the sensations caused by the concords of sounds are much
weaker than those caused by the sounds themselves.
But this need for a small room, which the name
" chamber-music " implies, is ignored, and there is
contentment with performance in a vast space where
the harmonies become feeble. The reason is clear.
As the relational elements are well rendered this deficiency of the sensational elements is forgiven.*

* Of course it will be said that quartets, &c., performed in
small rooms would entail loss : the audiences would not be large

17

Yet a further defect is produced in orchestral music by the supremacy of stringed instruments. Not only are the violins predominant in the sense that they yield the greater part of the sound, but also in the sense that their presence is continuous: they are always making themselves heard. The result is a lack of massive variety: there are plenty of small varieties, but not enough of large ones. That this is

---

enough. This is a sufficient reply from the *entrepreneur's* point of view, but the needs of musical effect cannot be satisfied by any such plea. My belief is that a composer would rather not have his quartet performed at all than have it performed in a way that sacrifices so much of its beauty. I am the more led to believe this on remembering that after one or two experiences I ceased to attend these performances: being dissatisfied with the general thinness and with the feebleness of the harmonies.

Here I may add that I have sometimes speculated about the possibility of fitting a room for musical purposes by increasing its resonance. If, as every one knows, surfaces such as those of curtains deaden sound by not reflecting it, and if, as every one knows, a voice in an empty room is much louder than in a furnished one, it is inferable that a room having surfaces which vibrate will give an increased volume to sound. Suppose that along the line of the cornice and again along the line of the skirting a rigid iron or steel framework were fixed with brackets at intervals, strong enough to bear a great vertical strain. Suppose again that pine boards, say nine inches wide and a quarter or half an inch thick, varnished so as to exclude atmospheric moisture, were fastened vertically between these two framings at one-eighth of an inch apart; each terminating in an iron clamp at top and bottom but independent of the framework, save by the intermediation of a powerful screw at each end attached to the clamp, and capable of being tightened more or less. And suppose these boards, strained by the screws at each end but otherwise free, to be also free from the wall: an interval of an inch or so intervening. Thus covering the entire surface of the room, these

a grave defect may be positively asserted, for it is deducible from a universal principle of art. Achieved by arrangement of contrasts, great and small, art of every kind forbids that monotony caused by the directing of constant attention to one element. Orchestral effects need much greater specialization. Sounds of kindred qualities should at one moment be used for one purpose and then sounds of other kindred qualities should be used for another purpose: thus differentiating the *masses* of sound more than at present. In fact, there requires a larger step in evolution—a more marked advance from the indefinitely homogeneous to the definitely heterogeneous.

Further contemplation of the contrast between the emotion produced by an organ and that produced by an orchestra, shows that a large part of this contrast is due to the far greater predominance which the bass has in the organ than in the orchestra. It is from the volume of an organ's deep tones that there comes that profound impressiveness which an or-

---

boards might, on the occasion of any approaching performance, be tuned by the adjusting screws, so that the dull tones they gave out when struck, though relatively deep would be in harmony with the tones of the instruments, and so that, by vibration in nodal divisions, higher notes would be yielded. The aerial waves striking them would be not only reflected back as in an empty room, but would be reflected back reinforced by the vibrations of the boards they struck. One who doubts the ability of the boards thus to respond, needs but to recall the ability of the metal disc of a telephone to respond to the faint sounds constituting articulations.

chestra lacks. As a masculine trait, deep tones are associated with power, and their effect is therefore relatively imposing. To show that this is so, it needs but to recall a part of an organ performance in which the upper tones only are used, to see that but little of the dignity and grandeur remain. Necessarily, therefore, in an orchestra, while the sounds of the violins are predominant, the trait of dignity is absent.

There is another way in which the bass-element is unduly subordinated. Besides having too small a share in the mass of sounds which constitute any complex composition, it is habitually excluded from the leadership. The theme is almost invariably given to the treble, and the bass is relegated to the accompaniment. This was not always so. In old times when, omitting folk-songs, church-music was the only music, such air or melody as existed was taken by the bass. Necessarily, indeed, this happened; since in those days it was thought improper that women should sing the praises of God in the presence of men; and it is not likely that there were boy-choristers. Even now, in Continental church-music, the bass takes a dominant part, and especially so in Russia, where unusually deep basses are in request for church-services.* What caused the change?

---

* It is narrated that one of these church-choristers, noted for his extremely deep and powerful bass, was once when travelling

From Sir Hubert Parry's work, *The Evolution of the Art of Music* (pp. 105–9), it appears that the growth of secular choral music was achieved by adding higher voice parts to these bass church-melodies: thus preparing the way for transfer of melodies to the treble. Possibly the eventual supremacy of the treble was in part due to the fact that, when rude forms of opera arose, librettists and composers were prompted by the sex-sentiment to give the leading part to the heroine, with the result that the accompanying orchestral music came to have a predominance of treble tones. There may have been a further influence. If, as is alleged, instrumental music of the higher kinds grew out of dance-music, then as in dance-music the treble, most expressive of liveliness, habitually predominated, this monopolizing of the leadership by the treble followed naturally. Be the cause what it may, however, assignment of the themes, or leading figures, or melodies, to the treble, has become an established tradition. May not this tradition be fitly challenged? Greater variety, greater impressiveness, greater beauty, might I think be attained by dividing the leadership, and giving the bass if not an equal share still a large share. Some illustrations may be named as justifying this belief. In

---

attacked by robbers ; but when he began to roar at them they fled, thinking it impossible that any one but a supernatural being could emit such sounds.

that charming old song " Pur di cesti," a fine effect is produced when, during an interval, the bass accompaniment takes up the melody. In the three *Contre-Tänze* by Beethoven, as arranged for the piano by Seiss, the first in quite an exceptional way gives the melody to the bass, and the effect is extremely refreshing. And then there is the third movement of Beethoven's C-minor Symphony, in which the prominent part taken by the bass gives a distinguishing grandeur, at the same time that it gives unusual variety. Is it not time that the feminine element should lose its predominance, and that the masculine element should come to the front along with it ?

Among future changes some old forms of orchestral music may possibly lose their pre-eminence. It is said that the symphony was originally a *suite de pièces*—the pieces being dance-music. Hence, considered as a work of art, the symphony has no natural coherence. Further, it seems that since in the choice of pieces to form the *suite*, the aim must have been variety, the successive pieces were selected not for their kinship but for their absence of kinship. Of course a like remark applies to the sonata, in which, also, the absence of kinship is conspicuous: instance Beethoven's Op. 26, in which the funeral march stands in such strong contrast alike with the scherzo which precedes it and with the allegro which

succeeds it. It may be true that in each such work a
design runs through the whole—that between the
beginning and the ending in the same key, the
changes of key to the dominant and sub-dominant
preserve a structural relationship; that the connexions among the themes are so maintained that by
the instructed musician a passage is recognized as
appropriately related to a preceding passage a hundred or two bars away; and that thus to a " high
musical intelligence " the coherence is appreciable,
and pleasure given by " the beauty of thought " displayed in the construction.   But here we have exemplified that misdirection of art before commented
upon, which makes intellectual interest a dominant
aim.   Truly artistic changes should be such as minister to natural changes of feeling, either emotional
or sensational, such as might naturally arise from
changes of mood.   Arbitrary ones, however skilfully
managed, negative that manifest coherence which a
work of art should have.

Are there not possible forms of orchestral music
which shall present successive stages in the evolution of a musical inspiration? Might not a piece of
such kind begin with a rudimentary figure occupying
attention for a short space? Then out of this might
there not come a slightly elaborated form, or rather
several such forms diverging in different ways, each
giving scope for varieties of orchestral treatment,

and such of them as were least successful being
dropped? Out of the best might there not come a
further elaboration, admitting of more numerous instrumental combinations; and again disappearance
of the inferior leading to survival of the most finished theme with its developed accompaniments?
Similarly by variation and selection might be evolved
a musical idea still better adapted to the sentiment
of the piece; and so on continuously. Meanwhile
by deviation from one or other of these figures or
melodic passages might come some conception so far
different in character as to furnish novelty of effect;
and this being in like ways developed through successive stages might yield the needful large contrasts;
and so on step by step until the highest development
of the composition was reached. Thus might be
achieved that coherence which, characterizing evolution, should characterize a work of art. There would
also result the heterogeneity which is a trait of development; as well as that concomitant trait of increasing definiteness, implied by the finished form
of the conception. At the same time the auditor
would have the pleasure of watching the gradual
unfolding of the composer's idea, and the successive exaltations of the sentiment expressed; while
the variety in unity would be step by step made
manifest.

Here let me close my heretical suggestions. In

music as in all other things the one certainty is that
the future will differ from the past and from the
present; and perhaps an outsider may not be altogether unjustified in suggesting what some of the
divergences may be.

DISTINGUISHED DISSENTERS.

" Force till right is ready," was a maxim with
Mr. Matthew Arnold. It expressed his general exaltation of authority. Curiously enough, along with
his recurring condemnation of " machinery " went
laudation of controlling agencies, which necessarily
implied machinery for achieving contemplated benefits. Hence his advocacy of an Academy. Hence
his applause of the Continental *régime* at large,
which is relatively coercive. Hence his implied
praise of a State-church notwithstanding his abandonment of the creed taught by it. And hence his
expressions of dislike for dissenters.

That this contempt of those who, as he puts it,
divide their energies between " business and Beth-
els," had some reason, cannot be denied. The dis-
senting world as a whole coincides in large measure
with the middle-class world, joined with a superior
part of the working-class world. Those included do
not display any of that culture on which Mr. Arnold
perpetually insists, but pass their lives in a dull un-
intellectual routine: not, however, as he admits, dif-

258

fering much in intellectuality from the mass of those
above them. Unfortunately for his argument, however, he has made a comparison, or professed to make
a comparison, between the notable men among
churchmen and dissenters respectively. I say unfortunately because, swayed by his own culture exclusively, he has recognized only literary achievements, or rather, achievements in that literature
classed as divinity: naming Hooker, Barrow, Butler on the one side, and Milton, Baxter, and Wesley
on the other: adding that these last " were trained
within the pale of the Establishment." (*Culture and
Anarchy*, xx.) But if any fair comparison is to be
made between Church and Dissent in respect of their
distinguished men, then men of scientific distinction
must be included; and if this be done Dissent comes
prominently into the foreground.

We have first the achievement of Priestley in the
discovery of oxygen, who, though he " builded better
than he knew," and did not understand the full
meaning of his results, nevertheless brought to light
the element which, judged by the part it plays, may
be called the most important of all the elements, and
who, beyond this discovery, added much to our
knowledge by his many scientific researches: being
also a man widely cultured in various ways, linguistic and other.

Next in order of time comes the Quaker Young,

who from his early days was an Admirable Crichton; displaying not only knowledge but originality of many kinds. In adult life his two greatest achievements, quite opposite in their natures, were decipherment of the Egyptian hieroglyphics and demonstration of the undulatory theory of light. That which Huyghens left as a hypothesis, he established as a demonstrated truth; and he did this in a manner so masterly that Herschel described his investigations as worthy of Newton. Equally in business, in science, and in linguistic lore, he was conspicuous—more conspicuous abroad than at home.

Out of this same small sect, the Quakers, came another revolutionary thinker—Dalton. Only vague conceptions about chemical combinations had, up to this time, prevailed; and though Bryan and William Higgins had foreshadowed atomic combination, it was reserved for Dalton to propound the Atomic Theory of matter. In conformity with this universally-accepted theory, all chemical investigations are now carried on, all chemical combinations and decompositions interpreted, so that there is no substance (excluding mere mixtures) which is not regarded as composed of definite proportions. Whether the atoms of which compounds are formed are regarded as actual units of different kinds, or whether they are regarded as merely symbolical, there remains in either case the truth that there is an exact equivalence between the amounts of different elements which combine, and between the components of their re-combinations. Dalton was elected, without his request, to the Royal Society and to the French Academy of Sciences. It should be added that he was the first to enunciate the law of the expansion of gases by heat, and that he pursued with success sundry other lines of research.

We come lastly to Faraday, universally known for the variety and importance of his achievements in physics. First there came his discoveries in electro-magnetism, and the induction of electric currents: the result being the establishment of that mutual relation of electric action and magnetic action which initiated the vast series of modern electrical developments. Then followed the reduction of electrolytic action to a definite form—the proof of the electrical equivalence of the ions of any compound decomposed. After an interval came the magnetization of polarized light, and the phenomena of diamagnetism: two openings into new fields of scientific research.

As implied above, the comparison made by Mr. Matthew Arnold between men of Conformist origin and men of Nonconformist origin, he ostensibly limited to those who have produced moral effects on the community. He writes:—

"An establishment which has produced Hooker, Barrow, Butler, has done more to moralise and ennoble English states-

DISTINGUISHED DISSENTERS.

men and their conduct than communities which have produced
the Nonconformist divines. The fruitful men of English Puritanism and Nonconformity are men who were trained within
the pale of the Establishment—Milton, Baxter, Wesley. A
generation or two outside the Establishment, and Puritanism
produces men of national mark no more."

Now even if we restrict the comparison in the
way Mr. Arnold does, it may be effectively contended
that towards moralising and ennobling English
statesmen the men he names have done less than
men of the class he derides—less than Romilly, who,
of Nonconformist (Huguenot) origin, initiated the
de-barbarization of our penal code—less than How-
ard, who did so much towards humanizing the treatment of prisoners—less than the three Quakers, Dill-
wyn, Wood, and Sharp, who began the anti-slavery
agitation, and, with the Sturges and others of the
same sect, greatly contributed to its success—less,
too, than the once-ridiculed but afterwards honoured
John Bright, who was an efficient agent towards re-
peal of the taxes on food, and was conspicuous as
the leading opponent of a war since recognized as
having cost much life and treasure to no purpose. If
any one looks for the ennobling and moralising effects of the bishops on the conduct of the House of
Lords, he will look long to small purpose; and, speaking generally of the lower House, it is manifest that
all the steps in liberalization, that is, towards nobler
institutions, have not proceeded from those brought

up under Church-discipline, but have proceeded, either directly or through outside influences, from men of Nonconformist origin. So that even if we narrow the comparison as Mr. Arnold does, the conclusion goes against him.

But, as already indicated, the strange fact is that Mr. Arnold excludes from the comparison all those mental achievements by which the life of our nation and of other nations have been mainly influenced. He says—" A generation or two outside the Establishment, and Puritanism produces men of national mark no more "—national mark being, in Mr. Arnold's view, estimated only by production of literature: scientific discovery being ignored. It is curious to observe what a blinding effect culture, of the literary kind alone, may have. For it would seem that Mr. Arnold knows nothing of those great revolutions in thought which, in the course of the last century, were produced by Priestley, Dalton, Young, and Faraday. Puritanism, he says, " after a generation or two outside the Establishment, produces men of national mark no more "; whereas these men were not only men of national mark but men of world-wide mark—men whose discoveries affected the mental careers of the scientifically-cultured everywhere, while changing the industrial activities of mankind at large. Consider what would be the state of chemical knowledge had not Priestley discovered oxygen, understanding little though he did the part it plays in the order of Nature. Consider where would have been the fabric of chemical combinations in all the enormous complexities it has reached, in the absence of Dalton's Atomic Theory. Consider what would be the state of astro-physics, and our knowledge of the constitutions of the stars and nebulæ, had not the undulatory theory of light been demonstrated by Young. And consider what would have been our ideas of the electric and magnetic forces and their connexions with light, had not Faraday initiated the theory of their correlations, and led the way towards those vast conceptions of universal forces which now pervade physical inquiry, as well as to those vast applications of them which are transforming industry.

Quite unawares Mr. Arnold, by the criticism he provokes, has done the reverse of that which he intended. Incidentally he has drawn attention to the astounding fact that, during less than a century, these four English dissenters did more towards revolutionizing the world's physical conceptions, and by consequence its activities, than any other four men who can be named.

BARBARIC ART.

A CONNEXION naturally exists between barbaric types of art and barbaric types of society. Autocracy is the origin of both.

As shown when treating of modern Imperialism and of Re-barbarization, both are concomitants of growing militancy; and militancy in its developed form implies coercive government. One of the accompaniments of despotism is display, serving to overawe the popular mind by manifestations of power of every kind. One manifestation is a gorgeous and highly-elaborated style of art—a style which suggests the thought of enormous cost and enormous labour, implying unlimited control over men. The earliest times show us this in the decorations of Egyptian tombs and temples, internally lined throughout with frescoes and externally covered with sculptured details of conquests; and the like traits may be seen in the remains of the Assyrian civilization. So was it in the past and is at present in all Eastern countries, where no form of rule is known

but that of the autocrat. Dresses crusted over with
gems and gold distinguish the ruler and his belongings, while his weapons and insignia of office are
similarly weighted with costly decorations, and his
gorgeously caparisoned horses and attendants add to
his grandeur. If we pass to Europe in early days we
see this display, implying possession of power, not in
court paraphernalia only but in implements of war
—suits of armour were elaborately inlaid with pre-
cious metals, while the surfaces of swords, and in later
days fire-arms, were covered with chasing. Everywhere costliness was implied, and hence expense
came to be the concomitant of high art.* Only with
decline of the militant *régime*, and correlative growth
of the industrial *régime*, did there begin to show
itself that relative simplicity by which truly high art
is characterized. A typical illustration of the change
is furnished by the modern preference for uncoloured
sculpture to the coloured sculpture and coloured wax-
work common in medieval days and in still earlier
days.

And now, along with that re-barbarization accompanying the movement towards Imperialism, we

---

* A striking illustration comes to me just before this page
goes to press. In *The Times* for March 7, 1902, the Japanese
correspondent states that a pair of silver vases, 15 inches high,
and inlaid with gold, to be presented by the Mikado to King
Edward VII on the occasion of the Coronation, represent "seven
years' work of 30 of the best Japanese artists."

see, curiously enough, a change of taste carrying us back to those types of art which were general in the days of coercive rule. First of all it is shown in that part of the social organization which everywhere and always adheres most strongly to the old—the ecclesiastical. The internal walls of cathedrals, which during modern days were plain, have been in some cases re-covered with tawdry coloured patterns; and now the ecclesiastics, having got the upper hand, are lining the dome of St. Paul's in the ancient style with mosaic pictures. Everywhere Protestant simplicity is being replaced by Catholic elaboration in the altar and its reredos, full of sculptured detail; and the vestments of ecclesiastics themselves have gone back to the old type—robes made weighty with glittering ornaments: all suggestive of medieval and Oriental pomp.

A kindred reversion characterizes our art-periodicals. Many of the things they offer for admiration suggest, at first, that there is taking place a violent reaction from the pursuit of the beautiful to the pursuit of the ugly; but contemplation proves that the ugly is usually the medieval. Here we see this or that artist's designs for country-houses and cottages, the merit of which is that they recall the buildings of past centuries. And elsewhere are views of interiors containing furniture utterly comfortless in make, but displaying one or other degree of antiquity

in style, and often archaic—often barbaric, that is.
In many cases grace and beauty have been positively
tabooed.

The same retrogressive taste various other periodicals display. Besides archaic decoration we see,
on the covers of magazines, a style of lettering distinguished from styles prevailing a generation ago
by its intentionally malformed letters, by the com-
bining of letters of different sizes in the same word,
and by other distortions reminding us of such as
might be found in the nursery: the irregular drawings of children and those of barbarians being naturally akin. It may be remarked, too, that in books
the titles are now frequently placed close to the top
and even in one corner—a deliberate abandonment
of anything like symmetry: not that abandonment
of symmetry which desire for the picturesque suggests, but that abandonment of it which implies disregard of proportion—lack of that perception of fitness which the geometrical form of a book dictates.
Along with this has to be named the reversion to
18th century type, giving to numerous books now
published the aspect of books published in Johnson's
day. Nay, there has been even a more marked reversion, as witness the much-lauded typography introduced by the late Mr. William Morris, who took
as his model the 15th century Roman type, and even
in part Gothic type, and who, in justifying one of his

usages, says—" This rule is never departed from in mediæval books, written or printed."

As displaying the process of re-barbarization in art carried still further, must be added the going back to hand-made paper, often specified in advertisements as a trait of superiority. And then the final abomination accompanying this, we have in the leaves with rough (" deckled ") edges. A trait altogether ugly and extremely inconvenient, impeding as it does the turning over of leaves, is named as an attraction by publishers, for no other reason than that it gratifies this feeling which re-barbarization everywhere discloses! Nay they go further. I learn from a paper-maker that " some publishers have the smooth edges [where the folding necessitates these] cut roughly with a blunt knife in order to imitate " " the natural ' deckle.' "

VACCINATION.

" WHEN once you interfere with the order of Nature there is no knowing where the results will end," was the remark made in my presence by a distinguished biologist. There immediately escaped from him an expression of vexation at his lack of reticence, for he saw the various uses I might make of the admission.

Jenner and his disciples have assumed that when the vaccine virus has passed through a patient's system he is safe, or comparatively safe, against small-pox, and that there the matter ends. I will not here say anything for or against this assumption.* I merely propose to show that there the matter does *not* end. The interference with the order of Nature has various sequences other than that counted upon. Some have been made known.

A Parliamentary Return issued in 1880 (No.

---

* Except, indeed, by quoting the statement of a well-known man, Mr. Kegan Paul the publisher, respecting his own experience. In his *Memories* (pp. 260–1) he says, respecting his small-pox when adult, "I had had small-pox when a child, in spite of vaccination, and had been vaccinated but a short time before. I am the third of my own immediate family who have had small-pox twice, and with whom vaccination has always taken."

392) shows that comparing the quinquennial periods
1847–1851 and 1874–1878 there was in the latter a
diminution in the deaths from all causes of infants
under one year old of 6,600 per million births per
annum; while the mortality caused by eight specified diseases, either directly communicable or exacerbated by the effects of vaccination, increased from
20,524 to 41,353 per million births per annum—
more than double.   It is clear that far more were
killed by these other diseases than were saved from
small-pox.*

To the communication of diseases thus demonstrated, must be added accompanying effects.   It is
held that the immunity produced by vaccination implies some change in the components of the body:
a necessary assumption.   But now if the substances
composing the body, solid or liquid or both, have
been so modified as to leave them no longer liable to
small-pox, is the modification otherwise inoperative?
Will any one dare to say that it produces no further
effect than that of shielding the patient from a par-

* This was in the days of arm-to-arm vaccination, when medical men were certain that other diseases (syphilis, for instance)
could not be communicated through the vaccine virus.   Any one
who looks into the Transactions of the Epidemiological Society
of some thirty years ago, will find that they were suddenly con-
vinced to the contrary by a dreadful case of wholesale syphiliza-
tion.   In these days of calf-lymph vaccination such dangers are
excluded: not that of bovine tuberculosis however.   But I name
the fact as showing what amount of faith is to be placed in medical opinion.

ticular disease? You cannot change the constitution in relation to one invading agent and leave it unchanged in regard to all other invading agents. What must the change be? There are cases of unhealthy persons in whom a serious disease, as typhoid fever, is followed by improved health. But these are not normal cases; if they were a healthy person would become more healthy by having a succession of diseases. Hence, as a constitution modified by vaccination is not made more able to resist perturbing influences in general, it must be made less able. Heat and cold and wet and atmospheric changes tend ever to disturb the balance, as do also various foods, excessive exertion, mental strain. We have no means of measuring alterations in resisting power, and hence they commonly pass unremarked. There are, however, evidences of a general relative debility. Measles is a severer disease than it used to be, and deaths from it are very numerous. Influenza yields proof. Sixty years ago, when at long intervals an epidemic occurred, it seized but few, was not severe, and left no serious *sequelæ;* now it is permanently established, affects multitudes in extreme forms, and often leaves damaged constitutions. The disease is the same, but there is less ability to withstand it.

There are other significant facts. It is a familiar biological truth that the organs of sense and the teeth arise out of the dermal layer of the embryo. Hence abnormalities affect all of them: blue-eyed cats are deaf and hairless dogs have imperfect teeth. (*Origin of Species*, Chap. I.) The like holds of constitutional abnormalities caused by disease. Syphilis in its earlier stages is a skin-disease. When it is inherited the effects are malformation of teeth and in later years iritis (inflammation of the iris). Kindred relations hold with other skin-diseases: instance the fact that scarlet fever is often accompanied by loosening of the teeth, and the fact that with measles often go disorders, sometimes temporary sometimes permanent, of both eyes and ears. May it not be thus with another skin-disease—that which vaccination gives? If so, we have an explanation of the frightful degeneracy of teeth among young people in recent times; and we need not wonder at the prevalence of weak and defective eyes among them. Be these suggestions true or not, one thing is certain:— the assumption that vaccination changes the constitution in relation to small-pox and does not otherwise change it is sheer folly.*

---

* A high authority, Sir James Paget, in his Lectures (4th ed. p. 39) says:—" After the vaccine and other infectious or inoculable diseases, it is, most probably, not the tissues alone, but the blood as much or more than they, in which the altered state is maintained; and in many cases it would seem that, whatever materials are added to the blood, the stamp once impressed by one of these specific diseases is retained." Here is a distinct admission, or rather assertion, that the constitution is changed. Is it changed for the better? If not, it must be changed for the worse.

PERVERTED HISTORY.

I BELIEVE it was a French king who, wishing to consult some historical work, called to his librarian: —" Bring me my liar." The characterization was startling but not undeserved. The more we look round at the world's affairs and the statements made about them by this or that class of people, the more we are impressed by the difficulty, and in some cases the impossibility, of getting at the essential facts.

I am prompted to say this by an extremely grave perversion of history, known to comparatively few, which I am able to prove in the most positive manner —a perversion which, grave though it is, would, but for an unlikely incident, have been incorporated in all future accounts of the relations between England and the United States.

Early in 1869 the unfriendly feeling between the two countries which had continued since the war of secession, was for a time much exacerbated. From the outset we had been reviled for not sympathizing with the North in its Anti-Slavery war with the South. It had been concluded that as consumers of

274

cotton our interests were with the South, and that we should necessarily, therefore, go with the South; and in pursuance of this conclusion, orators and journalists had vied with one another in their condemnations of us.

As foregoing pages have proved, I am not an unqualified admirer of England and English doings; but I was indignant that when England had, at the outset, shown more sympathy for the Northern States than she had ever shown to any other people —had exhibited a unanimity of feeling unparalleled in respect of any political matter, domestic or foreign—there should be perpetually vented upon her reproaches such as might fitly have been called forth by behaviour the reverse of that which she displayed. One result was that when, in 1869, the political horizon to the West was looking very dark, I was prompted to show the Northerners how wrong they had been in supposing that there originally existed among us that unfriendliness to them which we subsequently displayed.

I sent my secretary to the British Museum to look up the evidence contained in the London daily and weekly press, immediately before the outbreak of the war and immediately after. My remembrance was absolutely verified. Extracts proved that with one accord our journals of all parties— Tory, Whig, Radical—condemned in strong terms

the action of the South.   There were denunciatory
passages from the *Times* of Dec. 5 and 11, 1860, and
Jan. 4, 1861; from the *Daily News,* Jan. 2, 1861;
from the *Morning Herald,* Dec. 27, 1860; from the
Morning Post, Dec. 5, 1860; from the *Daily Tele-
graph,* Dec. 3, 1860; from the *Morning Star,* Nov.
27, 1860; from the *Express,* Nov. 20, 1860; from
the *Sun,* Nov. 19, 1860; from the *Standard,* Nov.
24, 1860; from the *Spectator,* Dec. 1, 1860; and
from the *Saturday Review,* Dec. 29, 1860.

Even stronger condemnations were expressed
after the declaration of war.   Witness the *Times* of
Jan. 18 and 19, 1861; the *Daily News* of Jan. 21;
the *Morning Post* of Jan. 9 and 12; the *Daily Tele-
graph* of Jan. 19 and 15; the *Morning Herald* of
Jan. 28; the *Morning Star* of Jan. 15; the *Sun* of
Jan. 19; the *Globe* of Jan. 14 and 18; the *Standard*
of Jan. 19 and May 2; the *Express* of Jan. 24; the
Spectator of Jan. 5 and 26; the *Saturday Review*
of Jan. 12 and Feb. 2.   Not a single expression of
sympathy with the South was discovered.   I heard
afterwards that in one monthly magazine, *Black-
wood's,* there was a dissentient note, and this was
considered a disgrace.

The above-dated extracts I embodied in a letter
to my friend Professor Youmans, and requested him
to publish it in the New York *Tribune*: hoping thus
to mitigate American hostility.   The letter was set

up in the *Tribune*-office and a proof sent to me by
my friend, with a request to withdraw the letter. He
said that adherents of mine who had seen it, were
unanimous in thinking that it would do no good and
would be mischievous by tying their hands. Though
I had expressed indifference to any evil which might
fall on me personally, I was, by this statement that no
good would be done, induced to yield, and the letter was
not published at that time. Some years afterwards,
however, when the ill-feeling had diminished, the
London correspondent of the *Tribune*, to whom I
mentioned the matter, asked me to let him have the
letter for publication. I did so and it eventually
appeared. There was an accompanying leading article referring in a slighting way to the evidence it
contained; and, as I gathered, though some effect
was produced, it was but small. Demonstration fails
to change established beliefs.

Several motives have prompted this narrative.
One is that though I have included in an appendix to
my Autobiography a reproduction of the above-de-
scribed letter to the *Tribune*, yet since most readers
never look at appendices, the rectification it contains
may have little effect. Hence I have decided to set
forth here the circumstances under which the letter
was written, and to give the dates of the newspapers
containing the passages quoted in it. Strangely
enough, even among ourselves the growth of the an-

tagonism, caused by undeserved vilification of us, seems to have obliterated all recollection of the original concurrence.

What must we think about historical statements at large? When twelve of England's chief newspapers, representing all parties, joined in a chorus of condemnation—when no newspaper was found which failed thus to join in reprobating the South—a conclusive proof of sympathetic feeling with the North was given. Yet in the North this conclusive proof was followed by diatribes against our assumed sympathy with the South. If this extreme perversion was possible in the days of a cheap Press and easy communication, what was not possible in past days when the means of spreading information were smaller and the hatreds greater? Beyond accounts of kings' reigns, of battles, and of incidents named in the chronicles of all the nations concerned, we have nothing to depend on but treaties made to be broken, despatches of corrupt and lying officials, gossiping letters of courtiers, and so forth. How from these materials shall we distil the truth? Judging from this recent case in which a grave misunderstanding between two nations was caused by complete inversion of the evidence, we must say that nothing positive can be inferred from the mass of passions, prejudices, interests, superstitions which moved men in past times.

The things that we can be certain of are happily the only things worth knowing. Through all these petitions, records, despatches, letters, &c., as well as through the laws that remain in force and those that have fallen into abeyance, there emerge numerous facts which there is no intention of telling—facts concerning the social classes, social organization, social customs, arrangements, changes: there emerge the data for Sociology, to which History, as commonly understood, is merely the handmaid.

WHAT SHOULD THE SCEPTIC SAY TO BELIEVERS?

To one who has relinquished the creed of his fathers there comes from time to time the question —What shall I say to those who believe as of old? To answer is difficult, since the reasons for and against this or that line of conduct are many and variable. Of course sincerity must be the dominant guide; but sincerity has sundry forms. There is an aggressive sincerity which seizes every occasion for trying to change others' views. There is a sincerity, less aggressive, which is ready to discuss, and to utter adverse beliefs candidly. There is a sincerity which enters with reluctance into arguments that disclose changed convictions. And there is a sincerity which is silent and even shuns the utterance of opinions at variance with those that are current. What attitude to take under these or those conditions is often a query not to be answered in a satisfactory way.

In many cases the Agnostic is misled by the assumption that a secular creed may with advantage forthwith replace the creed distinguished as sacred.

That right guidance may be furnished by a system of natural ethics, is a belief usually followed by the corollary that it needs only to develop such a system and the required self-control will result. But calm contemplation of men's natures and doings dissipates this corollary. It assumes a general intelligence capable of seeing the beneficial outcome of certain modes of conduct currently recognized as right, and the evil outcome of opposite modes of conduct; and it assumes that, having perceived the good results of this kind and the bad results of that kind, men will adopt the one and reject the other. But neither assumption is true. The average intellect can not grasp a demonstration, even when the matter is concrete, and still less when the matter is abstract. It cannot bear in mind the successive propositions but collapses under the weight of them before reaching the conclusion. Dogmatic teaching is alone effective with such, and even this often fails. The dogma " Honesty is the best policy," is commonly inoperative on the thief, since he always expects to escape detection. Further, the hope that average men may be swayed by the contemplation of advantage to society is utterly utopian. In the minds of those who form the slum-population and most of those immediately above them, will arise the thought—" I don't care a damn for society." And at the other end of the social scale, among those whose lives alternate between club-rooms

19

and game-preserves, there will arise, if not so coarsely expressed a thought, yet the thought—" Society as it is, serves my purpose very well, and that's enough for me." Ethical teaching, however conclusive, has no effect on natures which have made little approach towards harmony with it. Only the few who are in a measure organically moral, will benefit by its injunctions; reinforcing those beliefs which their conduct ordinarily betrays. Thus the Agnostic who thinks he can provide forthwith adequate guidance by setting forth a natural code of right conduct, duly illustrated, is under an illusion. By all means let us have a tracing down of morals to the laws of life, individual and social, and a continual emphasizing of the truths reached; but it must go along with the understanding that only as the discipline of a peaceful social life slowly remoulds men's natures, will appreciable effects be produced.

" Surely this amounts to saying that the old creed should be left in possession? Surely if the truths of natural ethics will, for the present at least, be uninfluential, those equivalent truths which have a religious sanction should be perpetually preached? Surely it is wrong to shake confidence in a theology which now exercises control over men?" The reply is that unfortunately the religious creed appears to be scarcely more operative than the ethical creed would be. It needs but to glance over the world and contemplate the doings of Christians everywhere, to be amazed at the ineffectiveness of the current theology. Or it needs only to look back over past centuries at the iniquities alike of populace, nobles, kings, and popes, to perceive an almost incomprehensible futility of the beliefs everywhere held and perpetually insisted upon: horrors like those which Dante described notwithstanding. If this lack of results be ascribed to the sale of indulgences and the assumed priestly power of absolution, then a glance at the condition of England after Protestantism had been established, proves that where such perverting influences were inoperative, the fear of hell and the hope of heaven influenced men's actions in an incredibly small degree. These threats and promises of punishments and rewards, appear in most cases to have done little more to guide men's conduct than would be done by a series of propositions showing that moral conduct is, in the end, beneficial alike individually and socially. Something rudely analogous to the law in the physical world that attraction varies inversely as the square of the distance, seems to hold in the moral world; so that proximate pleasures and pains, even trifling, influence actions more than immeasurably greater pleasures and pains that are remote. In a small way we see this in the conduct of the toper, who yields to the promise of instant gratification from more drink, notwithstanding the prospect of to-morrow's headache and sickness joined with domestic dissension and public discredit. Distant evils must be vividly represented before they can counter-balance enjoyments that are immediate; and in most people the representative faculty is feeble. Here and there are some of superior natures on whom the religious sanctions and reprobations so far reinforce natural promptings as to have beneficial effects. But if we recall the transgressions of adulterating tradesmen, bribed agents, dishonest lawyers, corrupt financiers, &c., we see that the alternative prospects of eternal torture and eternal bliss sway them but little. So that ill-grounded as may be the Agnostic's hope that a system of natural ethics will at once yield good guidance, it must not be inferred that endeavours to substitute such a system for the supernatural system with its penalties and rewards, will injure the average of men—may indeed benefit them, by showing the agreement between the naturally derived sanctions and most of those supposed to be supernaturally derived.

Moreover there are cases presenting to the Agnostic positive reasons for expressing his changed beliefs. For while on the great mass of people the current creed appears to be beneficially operative to a very small degree if at all, there are not a few on whom it is disastrously operative, causing by its threats great misery. To some who are sensitive and

have active imaginations the prospect of eternal torture comes home with terrible effect. Numbers of
them continue throughout life to be troubled about
their future fates; and in old age, when flagging vital-
ity brings more or less mental depression, this depression takes the shape of fears concerning endless punishment to be presently borne. In past times, when
" the wrath to come " was more strongly emphasized
than now, horrible conceptions must have brought
wretchedness to not a few; and even at present the
credulous to whom there is given some work like one
I have in hand, *Hell opened to Christians*, giving,
along with its denunciations, vivid representations of
various tortures, are sure to have days and nights
filled with ideas of sufferings without end. To all
such the man who has rejected this dreadful creed
may fitly give reasons for doing the like: pointing
out the blasphemy of supposing that the Power manifested in fifty million suns with their attendant
worlds, has a nature which in a human being we
should shrink from with horror.

On the other hand we meet with those who, more
fortunately dispositioned, dwell rather upon the
promised future happiness; and, by the hope of it,
are consoled under the evils they have to bear. The
prospect of heaven makes life tolerable to many who
would else find it intolerable. In some whose shat-
tered constitutions and perpetual pains, caused per-

haps by undue efforts for the benefit of dependents, the daily thought of a compensating future is the sole assuaging consciousness. Others there are who, borne down in spirit by some grave misunderstanding, look forward to a time when everything will be made clear and their grief changed into joy. Constant ill-treatment from a domestic tyrant brings to not a few unceasing miseries, which are mitigated only by the belief that they will hereafter give place to a state of bliss. And there are many who stagger on under the exhausting burden of daily duties, fulfilled without thanks and without sympathy, who are enabled to bear their ills by the conviction that after this life will come a life free from pains and weariness. Nothing but evil can follow a change in the creed of such; and unless cruelly thoughtless the Agnostic will carefully shun discussion of religious subjects with them.

What course to take is thus, as said at first, a question to be answered only after consideration of the special circumstances. The many who are reckless even of themselves and brutally regardless of human welfare, may be passed by; unless, indeed, some good may be done by proving that there are natural penalties which in large measure coincide with alleged supernatural penalties. On the other hand those on whom fears of eternal punishment weigh heavily, may fitly be shown that merciless as is the Cosmic process worked out by an Unknown Power, yet vengeance is nowhere to be found in it. Meanwhile, sympathy commands silence towards all who, suffering under the ills of life, derive comfort from their creed. While it forbids the dropping of hints that may shake their faiths, it suggests the evasion of questions which cannot be discussed without unsettling their hopes.

ULTIMATE QUESTIONS.

OLD people must have many reflections in common. Doubtless one which I have now in mind is very familiar. For years past, when watching the unfolding buds in the Spring there has arisen the thought— Shall I ever again see the buds unfold? Shall I ever again be awakened at dawn by the song of the thrush? Now that the end is not likely to be long postponed, there results an increasing tendency to meditate upon ultimate questions.

It is commonly supposed that those who have relinquished the creed of Christendom occupy themselves exclusively with material interests and material activities—thinking nothing of the How and the Why, of the Whence and the Whither. It may be so with some of the uncultured, but it is certainly not so with many of the cultured. In the minds of those intimately known to me, the "riddle of existence" fills spaces far larger than the current conception fills in the minds of men in general.

After studying primitive beliefs, and finding that there is no origin for the idea of an after-life save

288

the conclusion which the savage draws from the notion suggested by dreams, of a wandering double which comes back on awaking and which goes away for an indefinite time at death; and after contemplating the inscrutable relation between brain and consciousness, and finding that we can get no evidence of the existence of the last without the activity of the first, we seem obliged to relinquish the thought that consciousness continues after physical organization has become inactive.

But it seems a strange and repugnant conclusion that with the cessation of consciousness at death, there ceases to be any knowledge of having existed. With his last breath it becomes to each the same thing as though he had never lived.

And then the consciousness itself—what is it during the time that it continues? And what becomes of it when it ends? We can only infer that it is a specialized and individualized form of that Infinite and Eternal Energy which transcends both our knowledge and our imagination; and that at death its elements lapse into the Infinite and Eternal Energy whence they were derived.

Concerning the outer world as concerning the inner world, those who have not satisfied themselves with traditional explanations, continually have thrust upon them the same questions—trite questions concerning the origin, meaning, and purpose, alike of the Universe as a whole and of all its living contents, down to the microscopic forms of which earth, air, and water are full. On the Agnostic these questions are continually forced; and continually he sees the futility of all efforts to find consistent answers to them.

There is one aspect of the Great Enigma to which little attention seems given, but which has of late years more frequently impressed me. I refer not to the problems which all concrete existences, from suns down to microbes, present, but to those presented by the universal form under which these exist—the phenomena of Space.

In youth we pass by without surprise the geometrical truths set down in our Euclids. It suffices to learn that in a right-angled triangle the square of the hypothenuse is equal to the sum of the squares of the other two sides: it is demonstrable, and that is enough. Concerning the multitudes of remarkable relations among lines and among spaces very few ever ask—Why are they so? Perhaps the question may in later years be raised, as it has been in myself, by some of the more conspicuously marvellous truths now grouped under the title of " the Geometry of Position." Many of these are so astounding that but for the presence of ocular proof they would be incredible; and by their marvellousness, as well as by their beauty, they serve, in some minds at least, to raise the unanswerable question—How come there to exist among the parts of this seemingly-structureless vacancy we call Space, these strange relations? How does it happen that the blank form of things presents us with truths as incomprehensible as do the things it contains?

Beyond the reach of our intelligence as are the mysteries of the objects known by our senses, those presented in this universal matrix are, if we may so say, still further beyond the reach of our intelligence; for whereas those of the one kind may be, and are, thought of by many as explicable on the hypothesis of Creation, and by the rest on the hypothesis of Evolution, those of the other kind cannot by either be regarded as thus explicable. Theist and Agnostic must agree in recognizing the properties of Space as inherent, eternal, uncreated—as anteceding all creation, if creation has taken place, and all evolution, if evolution has taken place.

Hence, could we penetrate the mysteries of existence, there would remain still more transcendent mysteries. That which can be thought of neither as made nor evolved presents us with facts the origin of which is even more remote from conceivability than is the origin of the facts presented by visible and tangible things. It is impossible to imagine how there came to exist the marvellous space-relations referred to above. We are obliged to recognize these as having belonged to Space from all eternity.

And then comes the thought of this universal matrix itself, anteceding alike creation or evolution, whichever be assumed, and infinitely transcending both, alike in extent and duration; since both, if conceived at all, must be conceived as having had beginnings, while Space had no beginning. The thought of this blank form of existence which, explored in all directions as far as imagination can reach, has, beyond that, an unexplored region compared with which the part which imagination has traversed is but infinitesimal—the thought of a Space compared with which our immeasurable sidereal system dwindles to a point, is a thought too overwhelming to be dwelt upon. Of late years the consciousness that without origin or cause infinite Space has ever existed and must ever exist, produces in me a feeling from which I shrink.

(3)

THE END.